Everything

Anxiety Ever

Told You is a **Lie**

(*Well, almost everything!)

Dr Toni Lindsay is a clinical and health psychologist who has been working with both adolescents and adults for over ten years. She works at Chris O'Brien Lifehouse and teaches at the University of Melbourne (Adolescent Medicine) and the University of Sydney Nursing School.

Everything

Anxiety Ever

Told You is a **Lie**

(*Well, almost everything!)

Dr Toni Lindsay

First published 2024

Exisle Publishing Pty Ltd
PO Box 864, Chatswood, NSW 2057, Australia
226 High Street, Dunedin, 9016, New Zealand
www.exislepublishing.com

A CiP record for this book is available from the National Library of Australia.

ISBN 978-1-922539-99-1

Designed by Bee Creative
Illustrations courtesy of Adobe Stock, Vectorstock and Bee Creative
Typeset in PT Serif, 11pt
Printed in China

This book uses paper sourced under ISO 14001 guidelines from well-managed forests and other controlled sources.

10 9 8 7 6 5 4 3 2 1

Disclaimer
This book is a general guide only and should never be a substitute for the skill, knowledge and experience of a qualified medical professional dealing with the facts, circumstances and symptoms of a particular case. The nutritional, medical and health information presented in this book is based on the research, training and professional experience of the author, and is true and complete to the best of their knowledge. However, this book is intended only as an informative guide; it is not intended to replace or countermand the advice given by the reader's personal physician. Because each person and situation is unique, the author and the publisher urge the reader to check with a qualified healthcare professional before using any procedure where there is a question as to its appropriateness. The author, publisher and their distributors are not responsible for any adverse effects or consequences resulting from the use of the information in this book. It is the responsibility of the reader to consult a physician or other qualified healthcare professional regarding their personal care. The intent of the information provided is to be helpful; however, there is no guarantee of results associated with the information provided.

To all the Young People I have been lucky enough
to meet and spend time with. Hopefully together we
have been able to make things a bit less tricky.

What's in the box ...

Introduction

I am about to blow your mind (in a strictly intellectual, nonviolent way!).

Sometimes, the stuff that our brain tells us is a lie.

All those thoughts. All that stuff that happens in there, well sometimes they are lies.

Particularly when it comes to anxious thoughts and worries. They are usually lies.

And all of the stuff that your brain tells you is going to go wrong. That's almost always totally a lie.

Our brain has a job — its first and foremost job is to keep us alive. But, on top of that, it makes sure that we come up with thoughts. Lots and lots of thoughts. The guess by scientists is that it's about 6000 per day; I say 'guess' because as you can imagine, it's hard to count our own thoughts, let alone everyone's (some people say it is closer to 70,000 per day).

But let's say it is 6000 per day.

If you live for 100 years that will be ... (365 days x 6000 thoughts) x 100 years = 219,000,000 thoughts.

(BTW, if 70,000 thoughts per day is more accurate, the number is closer to 2,555,000,000.)

I don't know about you, but I can't even begin to make sense of that kind of number. But I do know that many of those thoughts will be unhelpful or untrue.

But there will be a bunch of thoughts that show up differently ...

»   the ones that tell us all the things that might go wrong

»   the ones that replay conversations over and over again

»   the ones that tell us we are too fat/too skinny/too ugly/too shy/ too loud/not right/too different/too strange (I don't need to go on — our brain does a good enough job of this by itself!)

»   the ones that make us feel scared and worried about the stuff that shows up in our world.

Some of these are okay. One of our brain's jobs is to help us problem-solve through life — and sometimes thinking of these things helps us problem-solve.

But when we are feeling anxious, or overwhelmed, two things happen:

1. More of these thoughts show up.

2. These thoughts become more intense, and less based in reality.

It's important that we recognize these anxious thoughts are usually lies.

They are the ones that tell us we are completely rubbish at things, that everything is going to be terrible, and that the absolute worst things we can imagine are going to happen.

Guess what? Everyone has these thoughts sometimes. They aren't wrong or bad. It's just our brain doing its job and trying to help us.

But feeling anxious is really uncomfortable and hard.

This book is about getting to know our brains better so when anxiety shows up, we can do something with it.

This book is about making friends with anxiety.

What is anxiety?

According to Dictionary.com, anxiety is ...

'distress or uneasiness of mind caused by fear of danger or misfortune'.

Helpful? Well, probably not. The simpler explanation is that anxiety is about being fearful, and that fear gets in the way of how our brains and bodies work. It sometimes turns up about particular things — for instance, people might be fearful of spiders or of flying and they might do a bunch of things to avoid having to manage that fear.

This isn't that common, though. Much more common is what we call generalized anxiety. This is the type where a person might be anxious about lots of things that show up in their life. It usually means they are worried about stuff a lot, and that their brain is busy coming up with all the things that might go wrong (sound familiar?).

Anxiety is a tricky cat! It can show up randomly or really predictably. It can be mild, medium, or crazy intense. It can be in your body, or in your brain, or both. Sometimes people will know what it is, but sometimes it can hide in plain sight and people won't even know that it is anxiety that is showing up.

So, what does it look like?

In our bodies it shows up in the way we breathe (quick, shallow, feeling like you can't get enough air), heart racing, head aching, weird stomach sensations (sometimes butterflies, sometimes nausea), sometimes muscle aches and pains, sometimes funny digestive things (like wanting to go to the toilet all the time). Some people talk about having a sense of heaviness in their bodies. It can make you feel amped up and high energy, and sometimes you might be so exhausted you will crash out.

In our brains it usually shows up as busyness — a million thoughts (usually about stuff not going well) spinning around and around. These can be hard to catch and sometimes people struggle to identify any one thought that is showing up. Anxious thoughts are awesome at sucking us into them (and the story that they want to tell us), so they might start as something pretty reasonable, but then quickly become loud and overwhelming. They are also pretty good at turning up in the quiet times — like when trying to get to sleep at night — and people often try to stay really busy so that they don't notice them as much (more about this later!).

Because anxiety makes our brain so busy, sometimes it is really hard to pay attention and that might mean we don't remember things so well. Most people, if they are feeling really anxious, talk about feeling overwhelmed and as if they can't manage things.

If we were to watch a movie of someone who is anxious, what do you think you might see? Sometimes it's really obvious — the person might move around a lot, fidget, not sleep, or be a bit irritable. They might seem to have trouble paying attention or be working really hard to make sure they are really busy or distracted. That person can also look quiet and shy — if the anxiety is about fear and avoiding stuff, people might hide themselves away.

Mostly though, it's not as obvious. Most of the anxiety that happens to us, happens in our brains. And we can be really good at covering this stuff up.

I bet you have had a time when you've felt really nervous or worried about something (such as public speaking) but other people wouldn't have had any idea. In fact, you might have worked really hard to make sure people didn't have any idea! You might have put on a bit of an act — you know the one, the 'I've got this, nothing to see here' act. But on the inside you might have felt like a swirl of feelings: lots of thoughts, your body feeling really weird and strange, and possibly you might have felt like you wanted to vomit.

Anxiety can sometimes be hard for us to see, both when it is happening for us, and when it is happening for other people.

A trip down history lane ...

Anxiety and a bunch of other things that happen in our brains are there because in the past they were helpful for us. Sometimes, it even helps us now — like when we have to give a speech, or if we're going on a blind date. But for us to understand anxiety more and make sense of it we need to go back — way back, like before the internet.

I want you to meet Jane and Ruby, cave ladies who are busy living in prehistoric times. They are good friends and spend most of their time hanging together —

that's when they aren't gathering berries, having babies and just trying to stay alive. See, the problem with being in the cave times is that there is a bunch of stuff that wants to eat them, and their brains are just trying to work it all out.

So, one day, Jane and Ruby are sitting around the fire, nattering about something. And then, in the distance, they see a tiger prowling along. They both know that when that tiger gets closer it's going to try to eat them, so their bodies and brains kick into gear. Their brains start running a million miles a minute to think of the right way to escape — do they stay still (freeze), try to take on the tiger (fight), or run away (flight)? For the tiger, the best thing to do is to run. But Jane and Ruby were just sitting and relaxing (kind of like being on the couch watching Netflix), so their bodies will have to kick in.

To make Jane and Ruby jump up quickly and run, something called adrenaline turns up and sets off a bunch of body systems. All the blood from their stomachs goes to their legs so that they can run faster — but this makes them feel a bit funny in the stomach (butterflies anyone?) and also might make them want to go to the toilet (like, right now). Their brains stop thinking about anything else other than the tiger — nothing else will be as important as escaping! Their senses will be more heightened, and they'll probably have a temporary boost to their hearing, eyesight and smell — you know, so they can track the tiger better. And, most importantly, in order to run really quickly their hearts speed up and they start breathing faster.

So when the tiger gets closer, they'll be ready to go — all systems ready and on.

If they need to run because, well, the tiger is going to eat them, then they're all sorted. Legs full of blood to run quickly, breathing higher and heart pumping! But if the tiger turns around and decides to go and eat someone at the next cave over, then all good: their bodies will go back to normal (it will take a little while) and they can go back to chillin' near the fire.

Except, when they go to go to bed that night, curled up on the animal skin, they will probably be thinking: 'Geez, I wonder when that tiger might come back ...'

Survival of the fittest

You've probably heard about the idea of survival of the fittest? Simply put, this means that if a species doesn't work out how to adapt to changes when they happen in the environment, then that species will die out! The species that avoid the risk — just like Jane and Ruby — will be the ones who are around to go on and have babies, who'll carry on the skills they have learnt.

Take Kate, the cave lady around the corner from Jane and Ruby. When the tiger arrived near her place, she thought, 'I really like the stripes and the colour of its coat.' She hadn't seen a tiger before and didn't know what to expect, so when she got really close ... well, you know, we don't need to get into the details. Let's just say that we are telling a story about Ruby and Jane instead of Kate.

So when Jane and Ruby next encounter something that is a threat, those same body systems will kick in, and keep them safe.

And then a bunch of generations later, here we are. Same brain (with a few little modifications) but a bunch of different stuff going on. Humans are social creatures (Jane and Ruby in the cave, but also us now, wanting to be linked up with loads of friends and being part of a group) which means that we work really hard to ensure we aren't excluded. Most young people I know (and lots of older people as well!) are really worried about how they fit in. Sometimes, this is a source of anxiety in itself!

We also learn lots about anxiety from the people we're around. So, Jane and Ruby's experiences are there, but so are the ways we experienced anxiety as kids, or the ways our parents and grandparents did. This can also mean that those people who are a bit more likely to experience feeling anxious might also have parents or grandparents who are more likely to experience feeling anxious.

Great! So, what's that got to do with me?

So, even though we aren't being chased by tigers anymore (unless your life is a lot more interesting than mine!) our brains aren't that different to Jane and Ruby's.

Our world is still filled with stuff that threatens us — just not in a chase-you-down-and-eat-you kind of way.

The threats we have now tend to be more psychological than physical (although not always). Now, it tends to be things like:

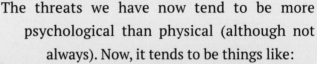

» worrying about whether you'll do well at school/uni/work

» worrying about what our friends think about us

» worrying about how our bodies look and feel (and what we think other people think about this)

» worrying about how we fit into the world, and whether we will ever find our 'people'

» worrying about climate, the world and all the hard things that happen in it (poverty, homelessness, war, etc.)

» worrying about our parents and siblings and how they are in the world

» worrying about whether we are enough

» worrying about whether something bad will happen to us (sickness, accidents)

» worrying about public speaking, talking in front of people or playing a game of sport.

And about a gazillion others.

Some of these might feel really familiar, and some might not feel relevant to you at all. That's okay.

The problem is that — thanks to Jane and Ruby surviving and passing stuff down — our response to these threats is almost the same one we would experience if something did turn up and physically threaten us. You've probably had this happen at some stage in your life — it could be as harmless as going on a rollercoaster, or much scarier (like a car accident). You would have noticed your body feeling weird (butterflies, breathing funny, heart racing) and maybe your brain either going blank, or having lots of thoughts about what to do next (both can happen!).

In our modern worlds this stuff turns up really often, and having a full body/brain response like this is really exhausting. So if it's happening all the time, it can be really tricky to manage.

(Just as an FYI, that's what this book is about: coming up with some ways to make this more manageable.)

Waves on the ocean

You've been in the surf, right? Well, if you haven't, let me paint you a picture.

If you go to the beach, and then go into the water, there are likely to be some waves coming in towards the shore. Those waves aren't always the same. Sometimes they're big, sometimes they're small. Sometimes they come quickly, and sometimes they have big gaps between them. But the same thing always happens: the wave builds (the blue-green lumps above the water's surface) and then as it gets closer to the shore it will break (the whitewash).

Then, by the magic of the ocean, that same water will be pulled back out and become another wave.

If you go for a swim, or even for a surf, you get to notice the ways that these waves move.

You can't stop the waves. They are just what they are.

But your experience of being in the waves would feel really different depending on where in the cycle of the wave you meet it.

If you are near the bottom, then the wave doesn't feel very powerful and it will just move underneath you.

But if you are near the top and it is breaking, it will feel really strong and overwhelming. When I have been in the surf this is the most terrifying part of the wave, and the part where fear really kicks in — this is the time all of your brain is screaming at you to get off the wave. But this is also the most dangerous time to get off! (Trust me, I have a gnarly scar across the top of my head from doing just that!) However, seconds after that, once the wave has broken it isn't that strong anymore, and all of that power has disappeared ...

You know where I'm going with this, right?

Anxiety is like a wave.

It starts off pretty gentle and doesn't have much hold on us. But then, if we get caught up in the thoughts around it, start doing things to try to avoid it or even try to stop it — it feels really powerful and overwhelming. In those moments of anxiety it can be hard to imagine that it would ever change. So, people then work really hard to make sure the anxiety never shows up again, or that it doesn't get any worse. So, they do things.

» They might be avoidant, so they stop doing the things they think are making the anxiety worse (like going to school or work, or seeing friends).

» They might try to numb it (by drinking, taking drugs, watching heaps of Netflix).

» They might try to distract themselves so they aren't thinking about it anymore (by keeping themselves really busy, and not allowing even a second to let it show up).

But what they don't do is let the wave pass them by.

White wash
Frothy hectic space.
Most intense part
of the wave.

Green wave
Building energy —
not powerful yet.

Easy to get off.

Broken wave
Heading to shore.

Way more chill.
Not much power.

Just like in the ocean, there will be a time when the anxiety feels really intense, but then just after that it will pass by.

And of course, another wave might come.

But if we are always getting off the wave when it is at its most powerful, we'll never get to understand what happens if it does pass. And you never get to nail your surfing!

Is anxiety bad?

Anxiety is a natural and normal part of being alive. If we didn't have any anxiety at all, well, we probably wouldn't get out of bed in the mornings. Anxiety is the same mechanism that makes us want to be successful, to achieve stuff, to feel good in the world, and to form relationships.

But anxiety is a bit like chocolate.

A little bit = awesome, helpful, can mean that we get stuff done even when it feels hard (like exams).

But too much ...

That's something else entirely. When we have too much it can start to interfere with how we are in the world, and get in the way of us doing the stuff that is really important.

There was a really cool study done years ago. They looked at people who were sitting university exams and how stressed they were about those exams. There were some people who were really stressed — maybe they had been up all night cramming, or didn't know the material that well. Then there were people who weren't stressed at all — cool as cucumbers, rolled into the exams, chill as. And then there was everyone in the middle — a bit stressed because of the exams, but had done the prep work and just wanted to get them done.

Who do you think did the best?

Well, it definitely wasn't the really stressed people. They were too stressed.

And it wasn't the cool-as-a-cucumber folks. They weren't stressed enough.

It was the people in the middle.

It seems that some stress in these situations actually helps us perform.

There are a bunch of things that will come up in life where it's really normal to be anxious/stressed/worried — exams are a good example, but there are other things like:

» giving a speech

» having a difficult conversation with a friend

» asking out someone you like

» meeting new people

» going on a trip by yourself (or to somewhere new)

» testing out a new language you've been learning

» learning a new skill

» having to deal with something difficult (an illness, someone who is sick in your family, changes in a situation)

» having someone close to you die.

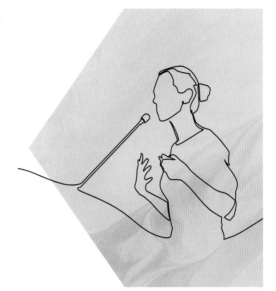

I'm sure that you can think of a million more.

Why it isn't about getting rid of it

You might think I'm a bit mad if I tell you that this book isn't about getting rid of anxiety. As we have chatted about, it is hard, and feels uncomfortable, and sometimes makes life unpleasant — so why wouldn't we want to get rid of it?

Well, just like we talked about in the last chapter, it's really normal for us to be anxious. And trying to get rid of it? That would be like me saying to you, 'Just go for a big run, and then don't breathe hard.' It's impossible.

I always think of the example of holding a ball underwater. Most likely you did this as a little kid. You go to the pool, and you have a ball you take into the water with you. It's really hard to get the ball to go under the water, and then it's really hard work to hold it there — you have to push really hard, and the force of the ball trying to come back up is really strong. But while your hand is on the ball, it will stay there. Say, though, you get distracted or you forget about it for a second, and you move your hand — that ball will jump out so quickly.

That's what happens with anxiety, too.

When you are working really hard to keep yourself really busy and distracted, and really focused on it, you might feel like the anxiety's under control. But then, whammo! It turns up just when you least expect it.

And sometimes, it will show up even when you are keeping yourself busy and distracted.

Sometimes, it will disappear for a while. And sometimes it will come back.

But think about how much energy it takes to keep the ball underwater. It's hard. You have to stay focused on it all the time. Probably, with enough time, your arms and body will get exhausted trying to keep it under the water. The exact same thing happens if we try to keep anxiety at bay — it's really hard work, and it will likely show up anyway. My guess is that you've tried all the things you can to get rid of anxiety, right? You're a smart human, with a brain that problem-solves! So, I bet if there was a way to get rid of it, you would have worked it out.

Instead, let's think about doing it a different way.

Who is this guy?

My guess is that this Anxiety Guy* in your brain looks like something.

It might be that they look just like you, or even a cartoon version of you. It might be that they look like something else entirely — another person, an animal, a shape, a colour, a feeling in your chest.

You might see them as words, or as thoughts.

It doesn't really matter — everyone sees them differently. Your anxiety will look different to mine, and to your best mate's. It might be hard to describe to someone else, but what I want you to do is to think about how anxiety looks for you. Through the book we're going to meet a bunch of the people that live in our brains — but first up, let's start with anxiety.

Take a couple of minutes and start building a picture of it: think about how it looks, but also how it sounds, how it feels, and how you know it has shown up. If you want to, you could even draw a picture, or scribble about it on a piece of paper.

I want you to hold that picture in your brain, and whenever we talk about anxiety showing up, I want you to picture that guy.

Throughout the book, we're going to get to know them very well indeed.

*I'm saying 'guy' here not because it needs to be male, it's just the way that lots of people I've met over the years have described the characters that live in their brains. I am happy for you to call it anything that you like (it can have any characteristics that feel right for you!).

The tug of war

I want you to think about a school sports carnival. You know the one: lots of noise, a heap of people running around, and if you're anything like me, you would have tried to avoid all of it! But there was always one event that I was into.

The tug of war.

It's great — a sport with the goal of getting others to land on their bums.

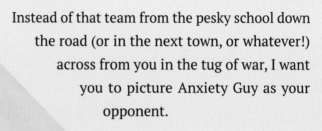

Instead of that team from the pesky school down the road (or in the next town, or whatever!) across from you in the tug of war, I want you to picture Anxiety Guy as your opponent.

There is usually one tactic people use in the ol' tug of war. And that is to pull the rope really hard and hope you're strong enough to pull your opponent over.

But we never tend to think about the other option.

So, think about your tug of war: you on one end of the rope, the anxiety on the other. You are pulling crazy hard ... but the anxiety is pulling back just as hard. It feels as strong as you are, and you are exhausted. That Anxiety Guy, though, when you look at them, they don't look tired at all. You feel like you have no choice but to keep fighting, even though you don't know how much longer you can.

Imagine what would happen if from nowhere you just dropped the rope.

You just ... let it go.

What would happen to Anxiety Guy?

They wouldn't go away — but they'd be on their bum.

But, much more importantly, you wouldn't be fighting with the anxiety anymore. You wouldn't feel exhausted from having to hold onto the rope so tightly and using all your energy to keep the anxiety away.

The anxiety would still be there. But you would be free to do whatever you liked.

And that's what we are going to learn to do.

Getting comfortable with discomfort

There are lots of reasons why people don't like anxiety, but the main one is that it feels really uncomfortable. It might be hard to be in your body when anxiety is around, and the noise in your head might feel too much to bear.

Sometimes we aren't very good at realizing that we are uncomfortable. Think about the last time you got really hot — my guess is that you got grumpy, and probably felt a bit jumpy or agitated in your body. Usually, we don't recognize that this is happening until after it has already happened. The idea of being 'hangry' is a good way of thinking about this stuff!

> Do you know how you would know if you're uncomfortable?
> What might be some of your early warning signs?

But we are clever creatures, so when discomfort arrives for us we usually have a plan!

As humans, when we bump into stuff that feels hard, our instinct is to try to come up with ways to get rid of the hardness. This is one of the reasons why we aren't living in caves anymore. It was a tough life and so we put our brains to solving problems so we could move out ... We started making fire. Then we could cook stuff and warm ourselves. Then we made tools in the fire. Now we could build some more stuff. Then we built better houses, etc.* You get the idea.

And this is the same thing we do now.

If we're cold, we put on a jumper. If we have a headache, we drink some water and take some painkillers. And when we're anxious, we work hard to make the anxiety stop.

The difficulty is, though, that getting rid of that discomfort is really hard. And often in trying to get rid of the discomfort we get more uncomfortable.

---

*Actual historical facts may vary. I'm a psychologist, not a historian, after all.

I want you to try an exercise (read through the whole thing, and then give it a crack!).

Sit down on the floor cross-legged (if this isn't possible, you could do the same thing standing up, or lying down). Set a timer on your phone for 5 minutes.

For those 5 minutes I want you to stay completely still. No movement at all (except breathing!!!). Notice what happens in your body, but also what happens in your brain. When the timer goes off, get up and go for a little walk around the room, then come back to the book.

How did you go?

My guess is that a few things happened. Possibly:

» you noticed that it was really hard to stay still

» your nose got itchy — like, really itchy

» you noticed parts of your body being really uncomfortable and you found it hard to think about other things

» your brain started to really notice the things that felt uncomfortable and then got really focused on them, and when you dialled in on them the discomfort got worse.

Any of those close? You might have had some other stuff show up; that's okay too!

How you thought the exercise would go might, I guess, impact how you felt about it when the discomfort showed up. If you thought it was going to be really easy, then when the discomfort showed up it probably felt really different than if you were expecting it.

The discomfort that shows up alongside anxiety is kind of the same.

If, when anxiety shows up, you are constantly trying to get rid of the discomfort, my bet is that it will be really present and it's going to be hard to focus on anything else. But if you recognize that it's okay for it to show up, you might not get so caught up in it.

Let's do an experiment.

> When the discomfort shows up, I want you to say to yourself, 'Ah. Discomfort! I've been expecting you. Nice to see you again. I know this is going to feel hard, but that's okay.'

How did that feel?

Nothing has changed, right? The anxiety is still there. The discomfort is still there. But you are less focused on it. And when you are less focused on the anxiety, you can focus on other stuff. You know — the stuff that matters.

Avoidance trap

The tricky thing about anxiety is it doesn't ever really let you win.

A good example of this might be when you want to go to a party. You might be really keen, but anxiety will show up and start chatting away. It might tell you that no one will talk to you, or that you will be really awkward and not able to keep a conversation going.

There is probably a conversation that shows up ... maybe something like this.

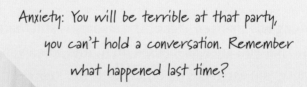

Anxiety: You will be terrible at that party, you can't hold a conversation. Remember what happened last time?

You: Fine. I won't go then.

Anxiety: Ah. Excellent.

You: Happy now?

Anxiety: Of course, I'll leave you to go back to your book.

When you give in to the anxiety it seems like the thoughts quieten down a bit, or it might even feel as if they've gone away. You'll text your friend and tell them you aren't coming (you might even have had to make something up). You know that your friend is bummed.

And you're bummed too — but the anxiety makes it feel too hard to do it.

So you sit in your room reading your book, trying not to scroll to see what's happening at the party.

And then another guy shows up ...

Guilt: I can't believe you didn't go to that party.
This is the kind of thing you always do.

And another one.

Shame: You can't even manage a party — you are so hopeless.

And another one.

Sadness: You've missed out on all these awesome things. Look how happy everyone looks.

And probably a million more.

That's what I mean about not being able to win with anxiety. There will always be something else show up.

But that's not all.

You know how we were talking about the wave before? Well, what happens when you avoid something is that, the next time you go to do it, it feels even bigger than before.

Say you are due to give a speech about something. You are prepared, but you feel uber anxious before it. It's at 10 a.m., and you realize that if you just go home sick you won't have to do it. The anxiety has probably even made you feel sick — lots of butterflies and nausea, maybe even a headache.

You feel sick, and it's legit to go home. So that's what you do.

The second you walk out the door, you notice the anxiety feels better. By the time you get home, you don't feel anxious at all.

But then, later that night, you realize you will have to give the speech the next morning. And that sick feeling comes back. Even worse than before.

When you wake up the next morning the anxiety feels so out of control you can't possibly go in to do the talk.

And when you make the decision not to go, the anxiety goes away again.

Until later that night … you get where I am going here, don't you?

See, the anxiety is being tricky — but it is a false economy.* Because if you'd just done the speech then and there, you would have been anxious, sure. But then you would have done it, and felt awesome for doing it!

And just like with our wave, when you go home sick, you're getting off the anxiety wave at the time when it is at its worst. So you never get to see that it improves if you sit with it (even though it feels gross) and eventually will dissipate.

If you aren't going to win, then it makes more sense not to play the game, right? Anxiety will constantly try to trick you into doing the thing that it wants, and then it will turn it around and make it feel like it's your fault. That's like playing a game of Monopoly with that cousin who was always the banker and somehow always won ... (geez, I wonder how?).

To not play the anxiety game we have to take the harder path — not the one that seems like the easy path (the avoidance path). Instead, we have to go bush bashing! (This will make sense in the next chapter, I promise.)

*A false economy is something that seems like it makes sense, but it doesn't if you really think about it.

Taking the dirt track

Think about the last time you went on a big road trip somewhere.

You would have filled up the car with a million things (most of which you wouldn't end up using!) and then left home, gone to the petrol station and got on the highway. Depending on where you were going to and from, you might not have needed to leave those big smooth roads. Those roads are great, because you can drive fast, the traffic moves well, and it's a bit like being on autopilot.

But maybe, you were going to stay at a beach campsite. That would mean you'd need to leave the highway and probably drive on a smaller road. And then maybe, you ended up having to drive on a little bumpy dirt track that made you move around so much on the seat you thought you were going to smash your head on the roof. It would have been dusty, and the car wouldn't have liked it.

But when you got there, there would have been an awesome beach in front of you without many people.

It was totally worth the dirt track.

And when you have to go home, you don't even notice the bumps so much.

Highways are highways because they are the paths that are most often used. They move food and people and stuff around all the time. But the bumpy dirt tracks? Not many people use these, so they don't get the upkeep.

The same things happen in our brains.

Our brains contain millions of connected pathways. The ones we use all the time are big and busy, like highways, with a bunch of information going back and forth all the time. But there are a bunch of other ones, some little roads and some little dusty tracks, that don't get much use.

The cool thing about our brains is that they are crazy adaptable.

If you start using a pathway lots, it will turn into a highway. And the highways you don't use much will get smaller and smaller and turn into dirt tracks.

So, at the moment the avoidance path is the highway — maybe even a super highway! It's really easy for your brain to get pulled into the anxiety patterns and the ways of anxiety. So every time anxiety shows up, it's easy for it to take that highway. If the way you manage anxiety is to avoid it, then it will go there really easily. And when you try to do anything else it's going to feel really hard.

But because our brains shift and change all the time, if you take the hard path a couple of times — even though you have to knock some trees out of the way, and it will be heaps less comfortable — it won't take very long before that becomes the easier road.

So, let's use the example from before.

Instead of letting anxiety run the show, you stay and do the speech. That feels uncomfortable, and the anxiety will feel really high and overwhelming. But then you will finish the talk, and feel awesome (you did it!).

The next time this kind of thing comes up, a couple of things will happen:

» You have already bashed your way through the trees and along the dirt track. So next time you do it, it will feel a bit easier.

» Your brain now has an alternative path. Before, it thought the highway was the only way; you have shown it that there are other tracks.

» The place that you get to is awesome — and sometimes the hardest-to-get-to places are the best!

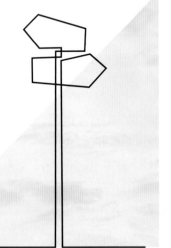

» We are learning machines — your brain will replace the old path with the new one, which means the anxiety gets smaller and smaller over time.

Let's go inside our brains

Don't worry. This isn't a science lesson. But it is helpful to know about what is going on inside our brains. If we understand some of this stuff, it can help us better understand what's going on when anxiety shows up!

Brains are still a bit of mystery to us — they're these cool, crazy machines that keep us alive and keep us evolving and changing to make sense of our environment as it evolves and changes.

I'm going to give a quick and dirty overview here. (If you're interested in this stuff, I encourage you to go deep diving! It's really cool!)

Our brain has a few very important functions.

1. **It keeps us alive.** The bits right in the centre of our brain control the basic things we need to keep us alive. Stuff like when to breathe, sleep and wake cycles, keeping us the right temperature. Without this kind of regulation our bodies don't work at all.

2. **It lets us communicate.** Most of the ways we process language and communication happen in our brain (not with our mouth and ears!). There are whole centres in the brain that take the information that is coming in, decode it for us, and then recode it so that we have a sensible response.

3. **It lets us make sense of our world.** We might think that most of what we see and hear happens with our eyes and ears, but it doesn't. Most of how we make sense of this stuff is from our brain filling in the gaps (this is vision versus perception). So when you see a tree, you are seeing a tree, but your brain (not your eyes) will fill in 90 percent of the detail. It's pretty wild.

4. **Our personality and who we are.** This mostly sits in the front part of our brain (cleverly called the frontal lobe) and shapes how we show up, how we respond to things and how we process what is happening in our days. We know that when people have had lots of hard things happen to them, this part of the brain can have changes to it. This is also the part of the brain that helps us organize ourselves and sort out tasks (i.e. it's the bit that helps you do assignments, or complex tasks like driving).

5. **Emotions.** There is a special place in the brain called the amygdala. This bit is like the emotional epicentre where all our emotions, feelings and motivations come from.

There is a bunch more, but for what we are talking about, this is the key stuff.

Now, though, I want us to dial in on the amygdala and how it is linked to anxiety.

This little bit (amygdala translates to 'almond' in Greek) is generally a crazy important part of our brain. It acts as a gateway to whether we feel happy or sad, fearful or optimistic. It also looks after our motivation and seeking out rewards (which we are known to do — chocolate anyone?). One of the important roles the amygdala has is moving messages between other parts of the brain (including the ones about senses and sensations), which also means that feelings interact strongly with sensory things. It also helps us build social networks, recognize faces, and remember social connections that help us exist in the world.

Think back to our friends Jane and Ruby. When they were being chased by the tiger they would have had heightened emotions and a fear response, so they would probably have been highly tuned in to the weather on that day, or the smell of the flowers in the tree next to them. We know that when we are in a more heightened fear state we notice more about the sounds/smells/ tastes, etc. around us, and if we later experience those things by themselves, they can elicit a fear response (even without anything to scare us).

> When we are in a situation that feels scary, the amygdala will send out a bunch of chemicals and hormones to help us manage that situation.

You can imagine what might happen if our body feels that we are under threat all the time because the system is seeing threats, such as anxiety, in our everyday) — the amygdala is likely firing off chemicals for us all the time to try to help us.

We know that when people are feeling more anxious and overwhelmed, their brains tend towards thoughts that are less positive and optimistic, which is a bit of a trap. And when we are in that cycle, it can feel really difficult to turn it off.

> Part of what we're going to do as we work through this book is to think about, and practise, lots of the ways we can work with our brain to help us make the anxiety feel less big and hectic.

How do thoughts work?

We've talked already about the ways in which our brain works. But so far we haven't spoken much about thoughts.

When I talk about thoughts, I mean the stuff that your brain comes up with.

'I am so clever' is a thought.

So is, 'I need to walk the dog'.

And 'I wonder who's going to go to the party on Saturday night … ?'.

And 'I really feel like a chocolate bar'.

And 'I miss my friends'.

You get the gist. (I could go on for thousands of pages with examples, but I'll spare you that!)

Thoughts are really important. They allow us to make sense of the world and our role in it. They help us navigate big things and situations, but they also help us just as much with things like going to the supermarket. Sometimes we refer to thoughts as a 'mental representation' that helps you make sense of the world. Kind of like a map.

For some people, thoughts are like a picture. For others, they are words. And sometimes, people will hear them like voices chattering away in their brain.

Thoughts kind of run to their own vibe. They can just pop into our heads completely separately to whatever we were thinking about last.

You've probably had this happen: you're talking to someone about something, then from nowhere your brain comes up with a thought about something completely different. Sometimes these thoughts can appear to be really logical. Like you start thinking about a TV show you've been watching, then you get thinking about that person who's in it, and what you saw them in before, and then you might start thinking about that show. It is all linked together in a bit of a string.

Even when thoughts turn up randomly, they might not be 100 percent random. It might just be that the back of your brain has been working on something for a while and will pop up with an answer to a question you asked it ages ago.

There is an old story of a guy called Archimedes, a scientist. He'd been working on a tricky problem about trying to understand whether a crown

was 100 percent
made of gold, or
whether it was a fake.
But he couldn't work out
how to test it (keeping in
mind this was a good long time
ago — 200 BC-ish — and so not so easy
to just Google it). He stood and thought
about it for days, and couldn't work it out. So
he did what we all do when we're a bit stressed.
He went off for a bath. As he got into the bath, the
water moved, and so he had a realization! The thought
came to him, not when he was thinking about the thing, but
when something else triggered him to think about the thing.

> Thoughts will often form patterns depending
> on how we're feeling emotionally.

If we're feeling optimistic and positive, then the thoughts that show up will likely come in strings that are pretty positive and optimistic. If we're feeling flat and sad (or sometimes even just tired), the thoughts that show up are more likely to have a negative vibe to them. And if we're feeling anxious, the thoughts will likely be skewed towards fear and worry.

We also know that when we're feeling anxious, it can feel like more and more thoughts are showing up.

Because thoughts show up in our brains, we usually assume they are true. But this isn't always the case. Despite knowing that it might not be true, we will usually believe what our brain is telling us — because, well, it's our brain that is telling us.

The reality is, though, that thoughts are just thoughts. They are just strings of words or pictures that have shown up in our brain.

This can be hard to make sense of, particularly if those thoughts show up in a scary way (like they do with anxiety). They can be convincing, and even a bit seductive (they pull you into the thinking, even though you might see that this isn't helpful).

Let's do an exercise together to better get to understand that thoughts are just thoughts.

I want you to get a piece of paper and write down the first five thoughts that come into your brain. It doesn't matter what they are.

For me they are:

1. No one is going to do this exercise.

2. I'm hungry.

3. My writing is a bit crap today.

4. I want to eat more chocolate.

5. I forgot to buy tomatoes.

Now write yours.

In a moment, I want you to write the same sentences again. But this time we're going to help your brain see that they are just thoughts.

Instead of just writing down the thoughts, we are going to write them with the phrase 'I'm having the thought that' in front of them. Here are my examples:

1. I'm having the thought that no one is going to do this exercise.

2. I'm having the thought that I'm hungry.

3. I'm having the thought that my writing is a bit crap today.

4. I'm having the thought that I want to eat more chocolate.

5. I'm having the thought that I forgot to buy tomatoes.

Finished? Now have a read through them. Nothing has changed about the thoughts, but my guess is that you feel they're a bit less real now.

Rational switch

Our brain is a thought-generating machine. All day, every day, it is pumping out stuff.

I want you to do an experiment with me (read all the instructions before you get set up!)

1. Get yourself set up in a comfortable position — sitting or lying down is fine.

2. Set a timer on your phone for 2 minutes.

3. Close your eyes.

4. Now, try to empty your mind of all thoughts. That's right: for 2 minutes try not to think about anything.

5. When the timer goes off, open your eyes and come back to the room.

How was it? Did you clear out your brain?

My guess is that you had a couple of seconds where you could do it, but then pretty quickly the thought-making machine would have turned on again.

You might have even thought that you nailed it ... and then you would have been thinking to yourself, 'I've nailed it! I don't have any thoughts!'

Guess what! That's a thought.

The point of all this (apart from being an awesome way of practising getting present — we'll talk about this in the chapter called 'Right here, right now') is that we can't stop our brains making thoughts. And we wouldn't want to.

Imagine if our brains didn't make thoughts. All those thoughts that help us get out of bed in the morning, or help us think about our friends and what we like and don't like, would disappear.

But the tricky thing is that the more thoughts we have, the bigger the risk that some of the ones that show up aren't going to be accurate. And remembering what we learnt about how our brains work, we know that when we are feeling anxious or depressed we tend to have more negative or unhelpful thoughts crop up.

> The other problem with anxious thoughts is that they tend to be less based in reality.

An example. Let's say that you have to do a test, and you've prepared for it. Non-anxious brain will probably say, 'Don't worry, mate. You got this.' Anxious brain will probably say, 'OMG! I'm not prepared enough. And this is part of my final mark for the year, and if I don't do well, I won't be able to get into that course I want to do, and my mum is going to be so disappointed in me. I won't be able to buy a house, and because of this I will have to work in the supermarket forever, just like I am now. My friends have been able to do it; if I just worked harder I'd be able to pass. Now I've let myself down.' Or something in that general flavour.

Things move very quickly in our anxious brain. Some of that will be rational and make sense. There is some truth in what the anxious brain told us before: the exam is part of the final grade. And doing badly in exams does make it harder to get into courses — but it doesn't make it impossible. (As an aside, many successful people struggled with school/learning and had to take a different path to get where they wanted to go, including me!) But a bunch of the stuff that the anxious brain came up with in that last example isn't real. It's just that the way the anxious brain presents it to us makes us believe that it is.

Anxious brains are very clever, and sometimes we can end up believing the things they tell us.

Even if those things are a stretch of the truth.

Even if those things are just completely untrue.

Even if those things are lies.

Because remember, anxiety will often tell us things that are lies.

But how do we know? The problem is that when our brain tells us stuff we believe it. It's our brain after all. It's not like it's some rando pumping stuff into our brains.

Sometimes the best way of checking is to see whether the Anxiety Guy has shown up.

Can you see them there? Have a good check, are they hiding somewhere?

If Anxiety Guy has shown up, then we can assume some of the stuff our brain is telling us might not be 100 percent true.

We don't need to get caught up in arguing with our brain about whether what it's saying is true or not. But if we recognize that anxiety has shown up, and that the stuff our brain is telling us might not be true — well, that's crazy powerful!

We are all individuals!

It took me a really long time to get this, but apparently it's the case: the stuff that happens in my brain is different to the stuff that happens in your brain. Different thoughts, different emotions, different responses to things.

We all start with the same base model, right? But even as we come into the world, the way that each of our brains works is slightly different. You might have heard about the idea of nature versus nurture? Essentially, are we born the way we are (and that thing is fixed and unchangeable) versus are we a product of the things that happen to us (and we change and mould depending on what our world looks like)? The jury is firmly out (people have been trying to nail this for a long time, without much conclusive luck), but it seems that it's a bit of both.

We are born a certain way, with a baseline temperament and bunch of settings for emotions. But then we build a picture of our world based on what has happened before, the people around us, the ways we have felt when emotions/thoughts have shown up, etc. And then those things interact with each other.

So if you're born with settings that keep you as cool as a cucumber, when you bump into stressful stuff you're perhaps less likely to be overwhelmed than someone who has baseline settings that lean a bit more towards anxious.

None of this is good or bad — it's just the way it is. But what it means is that just because I think and feel a particular way, you won't necessarily think and feel the same, and vice versa.

As an example, let's think about the ocean (yes, I know, again!).

For me, I love the ocean — and when I get pulled under in the surf I don't feel too panicked. I know it will be okay (because it has happened lots of times before). But for you, this might look different. If you haven't spent much time at the beach and in the waves (even little ones), the same thing — being pulled under — might feel really terrifying and overwhelming. You might hate the feeling of the salt on your skin (I love it!) and when you find sand everywhere it might really annoy you (okay, so it annoys me a bit as well …).

What I'm getting at here is that just because I like and enjoy the beach, it doesn't mean I can convince you to like it too.

Sometimes, the same thing happens with our anxiety, our thoughts, etc. Because we see how other people are acting, and it seems as if they're thinking in a way that is different to us, we can feel as if we need to think and be the same way. We might not necessarily understand why they are the way that they are, but we might try to understand it, or even try to show up the same way.

There are a couple of issues here.

1. We never know what is going on in anyone else's head, in the same way that people don't really know what's going on in your head. Just because you're acting or behaving in a certain way, it doesn't mean that's a good representation of what's actually going on.

2. We make assumptions. We will usually assume that if we are different to someone else, we are the ones who need to change. So we might find ourselves questioning why we're anxious about something that someone else isn't, and then by proxy asking why we haven't been able to fix our own anxiety — you know, since they can manage it!?

So, in being able to get to know your own anxiety (and all the other stuff that shows up!), we need to understand that just because something shows up for us in a certain way, it doesn't mean that this is how it shows up for everyone. Or that how it is showing up for you is right or wrong. It just is.

> All of those things you've bumped into in life — they shape how your brain makes sense of things.

Just like with Jane and Ruby, and their experience of the tiger.

Just like the first time you did something really scary/fun/exciting/awesome/sad/hard.

Just like how the people in your world might have taught you to make sense of stuff when you were younger (which might look a lot like how they make sense of stuff!).

We know that there are some common ways that anxiety shows up, but everyone will have a different way of making sense of it. So get out your pen and paper, and start scratching down a list:

» How do you know that anxiety has shown up for you?

» What does it look like?

» What does it feel like?

» Where is it in your body?

» What happens before it comes?

» How would other people know that you are anxious? What would they see?

Getting to know this anxiety stuff will help us work together to understand the ways it shows up, and what helps you manage it.

But also, it will likely mean that you recognize it a bit more in other people. And that also means that things might look different than you think they do. (I'm talking about how we make sense of what we think is happening versus what is actually happening!)

The people in
our brain

A few chapters ago we started talking about the Anxiety Guy that lives in our head.

But the Anxiety Guy isn't alone. There's a whole bunch of these guys and they turn up at all different times, and tell us all sorts of different things.

I like to use this idea because it is often easier to make sense of characters in our brains than to try to understand how thoughts and feelings show up. Just like we were talking about in the last chapter, everyone has a different experience of how this stuff looks for them. If we can get to know the guys who show up, we can change the way we decide to engage with them.

Perhaps before you started thinking about this stuff, anxiety was just a thing that happened. It was a thing that was horrible and out of your control. But now, as we've worked through the book, you've started to make sense of it in a different way:

» You know that anxiety is normal, and it's a sign of your brain doing its job (it's just that sometimes it tries to do it too well!).

» You have a bit of a picture of why anxiety is showing up and how your brain is trying to help you with anxiety and anxious worries.

» You can see the pathways the anxiety takes in your brain, and why it's sometimes easier to have the anxious thoughts turn up than some of the other things.

» And, hopefully, you're starting to think about the ways that thinking happens (particularly anxious thinking!).

So it stands to reason that the better we get to know the Anxiety Guy, the easier they are to make friends with (more on this in a bit).

But we know that Anxiety Guy has mates, too. They show up with Guilt Guy. And Depression Guy. And sometimes Shame Guy. And if Panic Guy isn't busy, they might show up too.

And occasionally, Everything is Going Well Guy shows up. But they seem to be the quietest.

Everything is Going Well Guy — let's call them Chad for short — is the guy that stands at the food table at a party, looking at their food and quietly making conversation with the people who come past. They might even have an awesome hat on. But it can be hard to hear them over the noise of the rest of the crew.

Anxiety Guy is great at making lots of noise and making it all about them. When Depression Guy says something, it's all doom and gloom, but people get suckered into their stories. And when Anxiety Guy and Depression Guy get going together, geez, good luck shutting them up. The others might not show up often, but when they do, they say really tough stuff. The kinds of things that make it hard to ignore them. You know, the things that kind of punch you in the guts.

So if we think about the inside of your brain being a bit like a party — sometimes it's a massive thumping one, and sometimes it's a couple of people just sitting around having a chat with some music on in the background — it can be helpful to get to know all the people who show up.

Earlier in the book, I asked you to draw a picture (either on actual paper, or in your brain) of Anxiety Guy. Now, I want you to draw a picture, or build an image in your brain, of the other guys who show up at your party. Some of them might be:

» Depression Guy

» Panic Guy

- » Everything is Okay Guy (even if you don't see them very often, make sure you include them — no one wants to miss a party)

- » Perfectionism Guy

- » Procrastination Guy

- » Grief Guy

- » Nothing is Going My Way Guy

- » Happy Guy

- » Relax and Chill Guy

- » Shame Guy

- » Guilt Guy.

There's probably a bunch I haven't thought of — have a look in your brain and find the ones that feel right for you. BTW, if you want to give these guys actual names, like Thomas or Genevieve or whatever else, that's fine too!

When you have a picture of the party, I want you to imagine that you've rocked up and are looking around and seeing all these people. Some of them you know well, some you don't see very often, and some are complete randos. We want to get to know all of them a little bit better, so that when they show up we know what to expect from them, and we can predict them a little better.

You know, like the person who shows up at the party, eats too much and vomits on the lawn. Every. Single. Time. Let's say their name is Helix. Or as their friends call them, Helix the Vomiter. And Helix the Vomiter never misses a party. When you open the door, you see them standing there, a bag in hand.

Helix: Oh my gosh. I'm so excited for the party. I brought chocolates, chips and sausage rolls.

You: Ah, Helix. Of course. I've been expecting you.

If you know who's coming to the party, you can prepare better.

Just like when Anxiety Guy shows up:

You: Ah, Anxiety. Of course. I've been expecting you.

If you're prepared for Helix, you can put away the food because he's brought so much.

But it's exactly the same for the guys talked about before. Each of them will have something about them that allows you to recognize them better and do some prep work, so that when they do show up you can welcome them and make friends.

And let's face it. The guys in your head are not so likely to vomit everywhere.

Friends vs enemies

I don't think anyone is going to be outraged if I say that having a friend is probably better than having an enemy.

Friends are awesome! They laugh at our jokes (even when they're terrible). You can tell them everything, and they'll be there for you when things are crap.

But enemies. Man, they suck. We've all had these people show up in our lives at some point, and most of the time, the only thing that comes from it is that we feel exhausted and miserable.

That said, I want you to think about an enemy. It could be that person at school/uni/work/home who is just annoying. Or the person you have a serious grudge

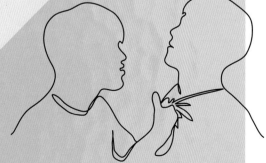

against. Or it could be the person who stole your lunch money when you were six years old. Or a boyfriend/girlfriend in high school. It might even be a sibling or step-sibling, or someone else in your family.

If you don't have an enemy (awesome, BTW!) that's okay; just picture something that really irritates or annoys you.

Have you got a picture of them in your head?

I want you to notice what happens when that picture of your enemy shows up.

> » What does it feel like in your body?
>
> » What shows up in your mind?
>
> » What are your thoughts telling you?
>
> » What emotions show up?

Regardless of the situation, my guess is that when you think about that person you not only picture them, but I reckon a bunch of stuff turns up in your head about them. Maybe you'll be anticipating how they'll act, or what you would say to them if they said a certain thing to you. You know how it goes — we play out all of these scenarios of the perfect thing to say (usually well after the perfect time to say them passes). And when that happens, there are probably some emotions that show up, too.

If you think about that person who's the number 1 enemy, you might feel:

» angry

» frustrated

» sad

» depressed

» anxious

» vengeful

» bitter.

The emotions that have shown up for you might look different, which is okay — these are just the most common ones. But you'll notice that whatever shows up, they are likely to be hard emotions — you know, the ones that feel uncomfortable to tolerate and hard to sit with. These are the ones that often make us want to do something. With anger, it might be screaming out loud or losing our temper. With anxiety, it might be worrying a lot and seeing the world as unsafe.

But what do you reckon your enemy is thinking/feeling?

Well, we have no real way of knowing. As we talked about before, what is in our heads is impossible for other people to see and know. But for the sake of the argument, let's play the odds:

1. They might be thinking the exact same thing about you as you're thinking about them.

2. They might have no idea that you have these thoughts and feelings about them.

In my experience, it is much more likely that number 2 is the case.

They will just be going through the world largely oblivious to the thoughts you're having about them.

And all of those hard emotions that we just talked about; you know, the ones that you're carrying? Well, they don't have them at all about this thing. It is you who is having to carry the weight of it all.

And you know what's even more wild? You are carrying all of those things … and it doesn't change what happens with the enemy at all.

They will still turn up to school/work/uni/home or wherever.

They will keep doing what they're doing (most likely).

This sounds a bit strange, I know, but I'm getting to a point, I promise.

Let's assume that you have a hectic enemy — she shows up in all of your classes, and she just gets under your skin. You don't know why, it's just the way it is. She hasn't said anything mean or done anything to upset you, really, but it's just the way you feel.

And so, every time you see her, you get angry. Like, really angry. You don't know anything about her other than that she annoys you. You have a couple of choices here:

> » **You can keep her as an enemy.** This means holding all of the emotion and hardness and having to fight against it all the time. Whenever you're in the room with her, your brain is doing a bunch of work thinking what you're thinking about her, and thinking about how you will show up, and maybe even how you think she is thinking about you. And then maybe how you will respond to

her. You might even be thinking about how you could get out of going to where you might see her, or how you could stop her turning up. You could spend lots of time having fantasies about getting her to leave the school, or her family moving away, or even how you could get her in trouble and get her suspended. Or you might be thinking about how she is smarter and prettier than you, and that it isn't fair that everything goes her way, and thinking about how much you hate her for all of that. Or you might be thinking about how one of your friends might like her better than you, and then thinking about how your friend isn't going to want to hang out with you anymore. And then you will probably think about that. (Wowsers, that sounds exhausting!)

» **You can work out how to make friends.** You recognize that this person is going to keep turning up at school, just as you have to turn up at school. And she will just be there. You don't have to engage with her, but you recognize that she might have something to add to your life. You realize that if your friends like her, then you might also like her. But you don't have to be best buds — you can just acknowledge her, and be aware of her presence without fighting against her.

The important piece of this story isn't about what the enemy does. The important piece is in deciding how you show up.

This might sound like a strange thing to say, but anxiety and this enemy are not that different. Think about the example above. And then think about anxiety:

» Both are showing up regardless of whether you want them to or not.

» Both can be tricky cats and might be doing
or saying things you don't like.

» You don't have any control over what they do — and
trying to control them probably makes things worse.

» Both might leave you sitting with those
hard feelings we talked about.

So, I want you to do an experiment with me.

I want you to picture your Anxiety Guy. Imagine they are sitting across from you, looking straight at you. Notice what their face is doing. How are you sitting? What is your face doing?

Now, I want you to imagine saying to Anxiety Guy, 'Dude. It's time for you and me to be friends. I'm tired of fighting with you.'

You might want to say it a bit differently (not everyone can imagine using the word 'dude' in a sentence).

What happened for you as you imagined that?

My guess is that, in naming the Anxiety Guy and then declaring the war over, you just bought yourself back a bunch of brain space.

We're going to keep coming back to the idea of making friends with this guy. But for now, you can imagine sitting with them, having a cup of tea (or water, or juice, or a cola-flavoured beverage), and thinking about how excited you are to meet a new friend.

What's the story?
The anxiety story!

When we run into difficult things in life, most of us work hard to get rid of them.

We talked before about how when you're cold you put on a jumper. That's a way of getting rid of discomfort (it's a pretty good way, if you ask me!). But there are other ways that aren't so helpful.

We all have anxiety stories. These are the stories we learn from the time we're little kids. And when we are kids our brains are like giant vacuums. We suck up everything — big lessons and messages from people and things around us, but also the little, subtle ones that you don't notice. These messages (I'm now going to torture the analogy) are like the little bits of Lego in the carpet. They're tiny, so you don't see them, but when you step on them, wowsers! That hurts!

We might learn a bunch of stuff that we don't even realize we are learning:

» The people around us might give us some messages that tell us the world isn't safe.

» We might have hard or difficult things happen to us, and so our brain helps us by making rules about what they mean (and what that will mean in the future).

» Our parents (or grandparents, or other adults in our world) teach us about how to manage emotions and feelings — the way that we manage them will usually look a bit like how they do.

Let's get to know how some of the people in your world might have shown up:

» It might be that your people have been **fixers**. These are the people who jump into problem-solving mode as soon as a situation arises. Sometimes these people will jump into trying to fix something before it's even really clear what the problem is.

» It might be that your people were **talkers**. These are the people who, when confronted with a problem, likely talk their way through it and express concerns or worries. This might mean these people don't follow through to action, but instead get stuck just talking about something.

» It might be that your people were **avoiders**. These are the people who really don't like the feeling of stress or anxiety (even more than the rest of us!) and will do anything they can not to experience it. This might mean they would have not addressed the concerns right there in front of them because they felt too big.

» It might be that your people were **compounders**. These are the people who, when confronted with a difficult situation, become so overwhelmed that their own distress tends to make the situation worse. If life was a cartoon and we were watching these people, they would be the ones running around trying to put out a fire while accidentally tipping the can of petrol onto it!

» It might be that your people were **deniers**. These are the people who push away any idea or suggestion that there is something to be concerned about. I think about these people as the 'nothing to see here' folk. This might have meant there wasn't any space for exploring or managing stuff that came up; instead, it would have been minimized or pushed aside.

Do any of these seem familiar? They might not, and that's okay, but my guess is that you can probably notice some of these things in the people in your world. And probably a bit in yourself.

Just as we like to understand the origin stories of superheroes (note Spider-Man and that whole business of the bite, and the absent parents and the grief of losing Uncle Ben), understanding our own stories can be really helpful in making sense of how we manage anxiety now. It also helps us understand when the anxiety is likely to turn up, and what it looks like in different situations.

When we are too close to something, it is almost impossible to see the detail or to look at it objectively. Imagine looking at a grain of sand under a microscope. You would be able to see lots of detail in that grain of sand, but you would miss everything else around it — the millions of other grains that make up the beach sand, the ways the sand moves when the water hits it.

This happens to us too. We see only the anxiety and miss all the stuff that happens around it (and that stuff is the really important bit).

Getting to know your anxiety story allows you to see it differently. This is part of the making friends process — we have to better understand all of the bits your brain has been filling in for you. We need to get to know how the anxiety first showed up, and what shows up around it.

Your brain might tell you that this is too hard or too scary to look at. It might come up with a thousand ways to try to avoid doing it. That's okay, your brain is trying to help you.

It's likely that your anxiety story will have a story of its own, where the anxiety tells you it is a bad idea or ridiculous to be looking at the anxiety story. That might be true; all of those things might turn up. But instead of getting caught up in that, I would like you to do an experiment with me.

Okay, so I want you to imagine with me that you are having to pitch the superhero version of your life. But to do that, you need to tell the origin story. This origin story is based on how you grew up, and how anxiety has shown up (and, BTW, the next part of the story, the bit we are working on now, which is how you have nailed living an awesome life, even when anxiety is around. But more on that later).

We're going to go hardcore scientist on your anxiety and drill in deep with the detail. We aren't going to make any assumptions; we are just going to notice what's turning up. We are going to ask some questions about your anxiety that you might not have thought about before. You might feel some of the anxiety rising and falling as you notice it — that's okay, it's just doing its job.

Below are some questions to help you get a sense of what kinds of things you might want to describe in your origin story.

If you get a bit stuck, here is one I prepared earlier. Meet Hugo.

> My name's Hugo, and my anxiety has turned up ever since I was a child. My earliest anxiety memory is from when I was six years old, and I was at a dance concert and had butterflies in my belly. Anxiety has been with me forever and I want it to be gone. It turns up whenever I'm faced with things that feel difficult or hard, but most of all when I go out with my friends. It feels like they are all doing better than me — at school, at dancing, at life. They've all started dating, and I can't even get anyone to notice me.
>
> My anxiety is a big blue ball of wool that sits in my chest and makes it hard to breathe. The wool runs through my brain and pushes me to only think about the worst-case scenario. It feels heavy. It is loudest when I'm alone at night, and it finds all the thoughts that I worry about and

plays them on repeat. It is quietest when I am busy — at work, or hanging with my friends. It doesn't go away then, but it is quieter.

If anxiety disappeared I would be relieved, but also a bit scared.

Now it's your turn to write down some things about your own experience. Here are some questions to kick things off ...

» When did you first notice the anxiety turning up?

» What was that first memory of anxiety? How did it feel?

» What is it like when anxiety arrives now?

» What does your anxiety look like? Does it have a colour? Where does it sit in your body?

» What kind of thoughts does the anxiety give you?

» Does the anxiety have a name?

» When does the anxiety always turn up? Is there something predictable or reliable about it?

» When do you get a break from the anxiety? What does it feel like in your mind if the anxiety isn't there?

» Imagine you woke up one morning and the anxiety had gone. What would look different? What could you do? What would you miss?

How was it to think about some of these things? Some questions were probably easier than others, and I suspect you learnt a few things about your anxiety that you didn't know before.

Most people only see their anxiety as bad and something they don't want. But I'm guessing that through doing this exercise you might have noticed how it is a part of you, and just like our superheros, having some of these bits make the character more interesting.

Let's face it. No one would care about the superhero who's been living a perfect life where nothing ever went wrong (*yawnnnnn*).

No, your story is way more interesting!

Hidden costs

So, anxiety isn't all wins (well, duh!). In the last couple of chapters we've spoken about learning to accept that anxiety is around and getting to know it better so that we can connect with it differently.

Fighting with it takes loads of energy, and so, if we connect differently, we have more energy for the important stuff.

But I can see that for most people that's a big jump.

Anxiety is really tough to sit with; it isn't as simple as saying, 'Well, then. If you just make friends with anxiety everything will be better.' Making friends with anxiety, accepting that it is going to show up, and recognizing that some of what it is telling you is a lie, also means bumping into some stuff that feels hard.

We talked a while back about the wave, and catching the wave in the right places. Right now, you're probably at the trickiest part of the wave. The bit right at the top, just before it breaks. And probably because you've been there for a little while, it will feel okay to be there. And anxiety is probably giving you a bunch of stories that show up to tell you that where you are is okay, and that doing anything else will be worse — just like the example before about not going to the party. In that moment, anxiety will tell you all the things that are going to go wrong if you don't listen to the Anxiety Guy.

But you know what the Anxiety Guy never tells you? All the stuff that you're missing out on by listening to the Anxiety Guy.

Here's a bit of a weird example. Think about someone who works at a shop you love to go to (it could sell clothes/books/musical instruments/terrariums/etc.). Say you go in and find something you want to buy.

You: Oh my gosh, I've been looking for this [insert whatever item here] for ages. I heard that you might have been getting some in. This is so awesome.

Person in shop: Really? You want to buy that one? It doesn't have the latest [insert thing] and it's made by unethical labour processes. You should totally go across to [insert competing shop here] instead. Also, that colour totally doesn't work on you.

Apart from not doing a stellar job on the sales bit, there are a few things wrong with this. The story that the person should be telling you is how fantastic the whatever is, and why you should buy it. And you would buy it, because that's the script. Also, I reckon this person's boss would have a little word with them about their sales techniques.

We have scripts turn up all the time, but most of the time we don't notice them. Like the scripts about social rules — we don't have to think about them, we just know them. Like not putting your feet on the table when you eat (or ever, really), or not picking your nose in public. Silly examples, but I think you get my point.

But think about the Anxiety Guy's script. It is in their best interest to make sure you're following their advice. So Anxiety Guy tells you a bunch of stuff to make sure that you do. Let's think about the party example:

You: I really want to go to this party.

Anxiety Guy: A party, really? Do you not remember what happened last time you went to the party? What happens if you make a fool of yourself again? You won't know what to say if someone talks to you. Some of the people from the uni down the road are going, and you don't know them. What would you talk to them about? And what if it's terrible and you want to leave, but you can't get home? What if you say or do something really stupid — you'll be really embarrassed and then you will have to go to uni on Monday and face it all. Also, I noticed that a pimple appeared on your forehead this afternoon. It isn't white yet, but it will be by tonight. Everyone's going to be looking at you. You hate it when that happens.

Anxiety Guy: Oh, you aren't going to that.

Alex: What do you mean?

Anxiety guy: You won't go. Exams are too scary. You don't know what the questions will be. The other people in the class have already studied way more than you, and so you can't catch up now. The exam will be hard — Mr Thomas is a tough teacher, and you're already struggling to do the homework. Anyway, you'd need to study for 8 hours each night to make sure you get the right marks, and you have all the other stuff to do. It would be easier to just not go to the exam. What will people think if you don't get a decent mark? This exam means everything.

Your Anxiety Guy might not sound exactly like that — that's okay, just think of what your guy would say. Here's what Alex's piece of paper might look like:

What is Anxiety Guy giving Alex?	What is Anxiety Guy costing Alex?
Reasons to not do the work, even though Alex wants to.	Some confidence about how Alex feels about the exam (they seemed fine about it until Anxiety Guy showed up).
A feeling of overwhelm.	Time to prepare (by taking over their headspace it's really hard for Alex to study).
Unrealistic expectations (if Alex doesn't study for 8 hours a night, they won't be able to pass).	Making it harder (when Alex listens to Anxiety Guy and doesn't go to the exam, the exam will still need to be done and when it is time to do it next time, Anxiety Guy is likely to be louder).

What is Anxiety Guy giving Alex?	What is Anxiety Guy costing Alex?
Panic (Anxiety Guy is making it sound as if this is the most important exam of Alex's life. It won't be, I promise).	Time to enjoy exams with Alex's friends (doing exams is stressful, sure, but there is something fun about the end when everyone is together and relieved it's over).

In fact, it seems like when we do this exercise with Alex, it doesn't sound like Anxiety Guy is really giving Alex anything. We could move all of those onto the costs column and it would be a bit more accurate.

What is Anxiety Guy giving Alex?	What is Anxiety Guy costing Alex?
	Reasons to not do the work, even though Alex wants to.
	A feeling of overwhelm.
	Panic (Anxiety Guy is making it sound like it is the most important exam of Alex's life. It won't be, I promise).
	Some confidence about how Alex feels about the exam (they seemed fine about it until Anxiety Guy showed up).
	Time to prepare (by taking over their headspace it's really hard for Alex to study).
	Making it harder (when Alex listens to Anxiety Guy and doesn't go to the exam, the exam will still need to be done and when it is time to do it next time, Anxiety Guy is likely to be louder).

What is Anxiety Guy giving Alex?	What is Anxiety Guy costing Alex?
	Time to enjoy exams with Alex's friends (doing exams is stressful, sure, but there is something fun about the end when everyone is together and relieved it's over).

Now it's your turn!

What did you find?

My guess is it would have been hard to start, but when you did there was probably a bunch of things that jumped out at you.

I want you to hold onto that list and come back to it if you think of other ways that anxiety costs you.

And we'll revisit this in a little while together, when we start to think about how we can tell that Anxiety Guy to pipe down a bit.

Is the story always wrong?

So far we've talked about the ways in which anxiety has been lying to you, and the ways it isn't helpful to listen to the Anxiety Guy when they show up. But what we haven't talked about is whether or not the anxiety is ever right (and therefore something to listen to).

So I'm going to start with a funny idea. You might have heard this expression before: 'Even a broken clock is right twice a day.'

In case you missed it, what this means is that even if something is wrong most of the time, occasionally it will be right. But what we don't know is whether that is because it's right, or because we guessed right that one time.

Think about that friend of yours, the one who seems to know loads about everything. Sometimes you'll be having a discussion about something random, and they will seem to know the answer to something you wouldn't have expected. It could be that one of two things is happening.

1. They genuinely do know about this thing.
2. They made a guess and got it right.

My guess is that same friend would then be very quick to tell you how they were right about that thing, and probably by extension make it seem as if they are going to be right about all the things!

This also happens with anxiety.

Sometimes anxiety is right. It might have been that you were worried about something (like failing an exam) and then that thing happened. But there is a bunch of possible reasons why you might have failed the exam.

» You didn't study enough.

» You were so caught up in worrying about failing that it made it hard to concentrate (anxiety running the show!).

» You were distracted on the day because on the bus on the way to the exam a commotion broke out because a lady thought someone had stolen her wallet, and in True Crime podcast vibe you were like 'Man, I gotta solve that mystery'.

» You had the measles, or some other infectious thing.

» You didn't understand the material to begin with.

I could go on and on, but I think you get my point.

But anxiety would tell you a different story. Anxiety would be quick to tell you all the reasons why you failed — and most of them would be about you, and how you aren't enough (or some version of this).

I don't know that we can ever really know what the truth is here. It is entirely reasonable that you didn't study enough, or that because of the anxiety it was really hard for you to focus. And anxiety will be really quick to tell you that it was right.

And so next time you go to study, the anxiety will show up, and just like that friend who is really confident that they know all about the thing, you will probably believe anxiety.

There is something in psychology that we call 'confirmation bias'. This is the idea that we put more weight in the stuff that confirms what we already believe. A really simple example of this is something we do every day on YouTube, TikTok or Insta — the algorithms show us things that we've already indicated we like (or stuff that's very similar).* We do this all the time in life. We tend to watch TV programs that are aligned with what we already think.

*As an aside, this is part of what makes social media so addictive! In showing us stuff that is aligned to what we want to watch, and making it new and exciting, we get totally suckered into the stuff that keeps coming up.

We tend to make friends with people who are pretty similar to ourselves in how they make sense of the world. And we like it when the referees in a sporting match do things that favour the team we're following (and if they go against them, we'll think this is somehow unfair!).

There is also 'hindsight bias', which tells us after the fact that something was obvious and predictable. For instance, the anxiety telling you that it was obvious you were going to fail the exam.

Anxiety uses both these things — confirmation bias and hindsight bias — to convince you that the stories it tells you are real, and that you need to listen to them going forward.

But let's come back to our idea of the broken clock. Just because occasionally the broken clock is right (well, twice a day!) that doesn't mean you would use that clock as a way of managing the rest of your life. You would be in all sorts of bother — can you imagine it! 'Ah, sorry, sir, I know I'm late for class. But this watch I have, well, it's been telling me it's 10 a.m. since 2021.'

I know. It's bonkers, right? But we do this with anxiety all the time. Occasionally, one of the things that you worry about will happen, and so we assume that every time we worry, it will come true.

We know that we can't stop the worries showing up, and we can't get rid of anxiety, but what I would like you to do is to press pause on the assumption machine. So when a thought comes up, I don't want you to get into an argument with the Anxiety Guy about whether the story is true or not, or whether you are going to believe it.

I want you to do that thing we have done before. When anxiety tells you a story, let's make sure that your brain sees it as a story rather than a truth. So, instead of, 'You are going to fail the exam', try, 'Anxiety is telling me I am going to fail the exam'.

How does that feel? Was it tricky to do? My guess is that the anxiety was pretty keen to pull you back into that story any way that it can. But with practice this is a really powerful tool. It allows you to see that, despite what the anxiety is telling you, it is probably wrong most of the time.

And the times when it's right? Well, we will come to that in a bit.

The drunk bloke
at the tennis*

I want you to imagine that you are on Centre Court at Wimbledon for the final. (You're obviously a gun tennis player, I can tell from here!) You are about to serve for the first set of the match, and the whole crowd has gone silent. All you can hear is your heart beating as you get ready to take the shot.

Except for that one guy. He's just behind you. You can't see him, but boy can you hear him. Every time you move, he has something to say.

*I know tennis isn't everyone's vibe. That's okay, just insert name of whatever sport/ hobby/setting you want. Just make it something where there is a spectator — applying this to you watching Netflix on the couch doesn't work quite the same.

Just as you're about to hit the ball, he yells out to you: 'Not like that, you loser, I told you to do it the other way. Bloody hopeless.'

And so you turn. And you see the bloke. He is the unhealthiest looking guy you've ever seen — his face is red, and he has two cans of beer lined up, one for each hand. You can almost smell the alcohol on his breath. He looks so happy with himself; he reckons he knows it all.

You're the one on the Centre Court at Wimbledon, and this guy is giving you tennis tips.

So you have a choice: you can turn around, tell yourself that this bloke is an idiot and go back to your shot (which you will nail, btw). Or you can go up to him and have a chat. You can ask for his feedback, and get him to explain the game to you.

Now, let's say that you take the second option. Do you think he's going to say helpful and productive things? There might be a couple of gems (see the last chapter re the broken clock), but it's much more likely he will tell you:

> » how truly terrible you are at tennis (even though you're in the Wimbledon final)

> » everything that you have done wrong in this match

> » everything that you have done wrong in the last ten matches, and

» possibly a rambling story about the history of tennis that you have no interest in and which is completely irrelevant.

Would that be helpful? Probably not, right?

But we let this happen all the time. It might not be a drunk guy at the tennis (that is oddly specific) but in our brains.

We all have the drunk guy in there. And he is chatty. He is quick to tell us all of the ways we're screwing stuff up, and that we are not showing up well. Most of the time we know that this guy is full of rubbish. But sometimes, particularly when we're feeling more anxious or worried than usual, or if we're more overwhelmed, it's harder to tell that guy to pipe down. It can also be really hard to recognize that it is him when your brain is noisier than usual.

Thinking about our Wimbledon example: when the crowd is really quiet it's obvious that it is the drunk guy who's making the noise. But when the crowd is noisy, it's hard to pick him out specifically. Just like how, in our brain when we are overwhelmed, it can be hard to tell who is making the noise and who it is helpful to listen to.

And what can make it harder is that the people who are saying the helpful things — like the coach behind you in the tennis game saying, 'You got this!' — well, sometimes in all the noise it can be impossible to hear them.

So, let's go back to our options with the drunk guy. We've already covered the first two — you could:

1. Ignore him completely and just get on with the game.
2. Turn around and chat with him (and get suckered into the story he's telling you).

But you could also do a third thing:

3. Acknowledge that he is there and then go back to the game.

It might seem as if 1 and 3 are pretty similar. But there is something really powerful in making the decision to acknowledge something. You are saying to the drunk guy, 'I see you, but I am not going to engage with you.'

If you just ignore him, he is likely to ramp up his behaviour and push things further so that you get suckered in. But when you say, 'I see you, but I am not going to engage with you', you are really saying 'I am being intentional about what I do with you, and right now I am choosing to not engage.' How powerful is that!!!

So let's see how this looks with anxiety (or other stuff that shows up in your brain).

I reckon by now you've gotten to know the ways some of these guys are showing up, or at least you might be able to notice when they've arrived. (If not, that's okay, everyone gets this at a different pace, and it might be worth going back and revisiting some of the earlier chapters.)

So, I want you to imagine that Anxiety Guy has shown up. And they have some stuff to say — lots of things, mostly about all of the things that are going to go wrong in the future. You have a picture of Anxiety Guy in your mind, and you might have even drawn a picture of how they look. I want you to imagine you are sitting across from Anxiety Guy at a table. They are getting ready to tell you all the things that are going to go wrong. You've been practising this conversation, and you know it's going to be hard. But you lean across towards Anxiety Guy, and you say, 'Thanks, Anxiety Guy, I see what you have to say, but today, I don't want to chat with you.'

And then you get up and walk away. Anxiety Guy is still there at the table, and they are still going to chatter away, but you've decided not to engage with them.

Phew.

I want you to notice a few things as you imagine this scenario:

1. What did it feel like in your mind and your body when you thought about sitting down and saying what you wanted to say?

2. How did it feel to imagine not having to engage with Anxiety Guy?

3. What did you notice about Anxiety Guy when you walked away? Did they get louder, or more insistent, or were they happy for you to walk away?

4. How might you be able to do this again?

Anxiety Guy hasn't gone anywhere. But now that you have unlocked this superpower, you are the one with more choice.

Just because the drunk guy is at the tennis doesn't mean you have to listen to him.

Thinking about thinking

This might seem a bit bonkers, but I want you to think about thinking for a bit.

Most of the time, the stuff that goes on in our brain is a bit of a mystery to us — thoughts and emotions and a bunch of other stuff shows up, and we just accept it for what it is. Our brain tells us something, and we just take it at face value.

But I suspect that you're starting to get a sense that this might not be quite as straightforward as you originally thought.

Just as onions have layers, anxiety has layers. This can be a hard thing to get your head around, but stick with me. Imagine you cut an onion down the middle (yup, that's right, I'm sticking with the onion metaphor). Right in the middle you will see the chunky bit — I want you to think about that as the thing you're anxious about (it might be an exam, pain in your leg, an argument with a friend, etc.). This is the concrete thing that we know about for sure. So it might be that you have an exam next week.

That's the first layer.

Then the second layer is the anxiety about the thing. So this might be those first feelings of anxiety that show up in your body or in your mind when you know that the exam is coming. This is the stuff that we've been talking about until now.

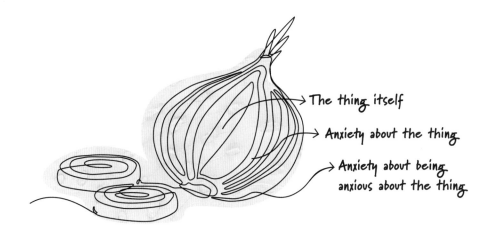

The thing itself

Anxiety about the thing

Anxiety about being anxious about the thing

Then the third layer shows up. This is the layer where you start thinking about the anxiety. And this is where things get wild. Because, actually, the exam, and the anxiety about the exam are both okay. The anxiety that's shown up in that second layer is your brain doing its job, just like the cave people's brains did the job of protecting them from the tigers. But the anxiety about the anxiety that turns up in the third layer starts to get into some tricky territory. This is the layer where you'll start getting anxious about the idea of the anxiety showing up. This is where the avoidance of anxiety shows up, and all of the things we've been talking about. Your thoughts might be telling you things like 'I can't handle this' or 'How come no one else gets anxious like me?'

But it doesn't stop there.

There is a fourth layer, where we start thinking about being anxious about being anxious.

And then a fifth, and a sixth … and it just keeps going.

> These things are called secondary anxiety, which means you aren't just anxious about the thing itself — you're also anxious about being anxious.

This isn't good or bad; it is just your brain trying to work out what to do with all of this anxiety stuff. But you can imagine that you can get quite trapped in the cycle of thinking about thinking about thinking about thinking.

Some people also talk about this as being 'clean thoughts and dirty thoughts' (no, not that kind!). The clean thoughts are the thing itself (anxiety about the exam), and the dirty thoughts are all the thoughts you have about that thing (anxiety about the anxiety).

We're going to talk about sleep a bit later on, but it's a great example of how this works. Say it's 2 a.m. and you want to be asleep. You've been tossing and turning for ages, and you've tried all the things that normally work, but for some reason you just can't get off to sleep.

The first layer (or the clean thought) is that you aren't asleep. Then the second layers (the dirty thoughts) are all the stuff that comes along with that:

- » 'I should be asleep.'

- » 'I have to go to school/work/uni tomorrow and I'm going to be so tired.'

- » 'I hate that I'm not sleeping.'

The third layers (also dirty thoughts) are then the thinking about the thinking:

- » 'I'm a failure for not being able to stop my thinking about this so that I can go to sleep.'

- » 'If I was better able to manage my life, I would be able to sleep better.'

You might be wondering what the point of all this is.

Well, it's really important to notice the ways that our thoughts show up, and the ways that we can sometimes get caught up in the thinking about the things rather than being present to what is actually in the here and now.

But, more importantly, we've realized that we can't do much to stop anxiety showing up, but we can do some work on how we think about the anxiety that shows up. You've already been doing a bunch of this as you've worked through the book, but there is a still a bit more to do.

The A word

Nah, not that one. And not anxiety either.

We are going to talk about acceptance (the other, other A word).

My guess is that you already have some ideas about what acceptance might mean — and particularly when we are talking about thoughts and emotions. Almost everyone I meet will have these thoughts, and they are almost always the same. They will say something to me like ... 'So, I just need to suck it up' or 'There isn't anything I can do about it, and so, what's the point?'

And I'm guessing that those might be the thoughts that show up for you as well.

But here's the thing. Acceptance isn't about the thing itself, it's about what shows up around the thing (just like our onion example). And, let's face it, some things in life are just rubbish, and no amount of thinking about accepting them will feel okay.

Think about something terrible happening — a big natural disaster where people die or lose their houses, or a war, or getting sick. We know that these things are big and hard and will change the course of people's lives forever, and I don't think we would ever say to someone, 'Hey mate, suck it up, what are you whinging about?' (Well, I hope not at least.)

Or maybe it isn't something that terrible, but something that feels really terrible. Breaking up with someone. Failing an exam. Having a big fight with a friend. If these things were happening to someone, you probably wouldn't tell them to suck it up and get on with it either.

But somehow we do this to ourselves all the time. We expect that we will be fine, even when hard things happen. So when something hard comes along, and we have a response to it — it might be sadness, or anger, or frustration — we will usually try to get rid of that feeling (we have talked about this loads), and one of the ways we do this is we tell ourselves to 'suck it up' and undervalue what our brain is trying to tell us.

It's totally reasonable to feel things. And it's okay that those things feel hard.

I'm going to say that again – because it's really important.

> It's totally reasonable to feel things. And it's okay that those things feel hard.

Because of how movies are (and a bunch of other stuff) we often tell ourselves that if we aren't happy all the time this is some type of failure. But the opposite is true. Our lives are hard — we have to struggle against a bunch of things, and stuff won't always go our way.

One of the things we've been doing as we've walked through the book is to look at the ways our brains show up to these hard things (like anxiety) and how we can do some work to help make these more manageable. We're now going to unlock a key bit of this. That's the acceptance bit.

I want you to think about the last time something hard happened (it can be big or small) and I want you to write down what you did when that happened. Here are some examples; read through these first, then copy the headings below and get scribbling!

What happened?	Had a big fight with a friend.
What happened in your body?	Heart racing, felt sick.
What happened in your brain?	Anxiety showed up. I felt scared and worried that she would never talk to me again. I had lots of thoughts about how I'm a loser.
What did you do?	Distracted myself — numbed out by watching hours of YouTube. Didn't do my homework.
How did it feel when you did that?	Better — for a while, but then when I stopped, the thoughts were still there, and I was still sad. It felt worse.

How did you go? Did your example look similar to the one above, where in trying to make things better (and by avoiding the hard feelings) things actually ended up feeling worse?

I wonder what it would look like if we changed this process a bit.

I want you to think about how you can show up to this differently. See, this stuff is really predictable. We know that when hard stuff shows up (big or small), hard emotions will show up as well. We don't want to get rid of them, but just like we made friends with anxiety earlier in the book we're going to do the same thing with those emotions. Instead of trying to push them away, we're going to welcome them in for a cup of tea.

So, the conversation before might have looked like this:

You: I'm really scared that Josie will never talk to me again.

Anxiety: Yup! Here I am! I have a story for you. Of course, Josie won't ever talk to you again, you're a loser. I can't believe you did that thing to her.

You: Go away, anxiety!

Anxiety: You're kidding me, aren't you? I'm not going anywhere! Loser, loser, loser, loser.

You: [Turns on YouTube and tries to not notice all the stuff that is showing up in your brain.]

Your conversation will look different, of course. But what if we see the anxiety (or whatever else shows up) as a friend rather than something to get rid of? What if we bring acceptance to the party?

If we do that, the conversation might be:

You: I'm really scared that Josie will never talk to me again.

Anxiety: Yup! Here I am! I have a story for you. Of course, Josie won't ever talk to you again, you're a loser. I can't believe you did that thing to her.

You: Ah, anxiety. I've been expecting you. You always show up when tough things happen.

Anxiety: What?!? No, listen to this story I have to tell you. Didn't you hear me? I told you, you're such a loser and Josie will never talk to you again.

You: Anxiety, it's okay. Like I said, I was expecting you. It's okay. I am meant to be anxious right now.

I'm sure that this conversation could go on and on. And just like when we've done these things before, you might have noticed that the anxiety hasn't gone anywhere.

We haven't fixed it.

And we haven't tried to change it.

Or argue with it.

Or try to make it agree with you.

things that went wrong, that weren't okay, and all the things that have felt terrible.

But when we are driving, the most important thing is to be focused on the here and now (at least if you don't want to have accidents!). All the uncertainty and anxiety in our world lives in the future, and we get caught up in trying to think about all the ways that things will happen. As we have chatted about through the book, thinking about the future is no guarantee that what you are thinking about is going to happen (in fact, the stuff we are worried about almost never happens).

So, you know what the antidote to this is? It's to be present right now. In this moment.

Now, I am not talking monk-on-the-mountain present, meditating in the snow for hours at a time (I mean, you can if you want!). I am thinking much more about simple 5-second things you can do that pull you out of what's going on in your brain, and bring you back to the here and now.

And guess what? There is a bunch of research that shows that being present and being intentional about practising being present impacts how we manage stress and what shows up for us when we bump into difficult stuff.

Get with the breathing!

These are exercises that bring your attention to your breath. One of the ones I've found most helpful for people is to do a 6-second breathing cycle: breathe in for 3 seconds, then breathe out for 3 seconds. You can do this ten times, which will take about a minute. Counting helps keep you engaged in the process and helps your mind to not wander and stay present with the exercise.

Another activity that works quite well is breathing in as deeply as you can for 5 seconds and then breathing out as much as you can for 5 seconds. This might feel a bit uncomfortable as you notice the feeling of filling and emptying your lungs. That's okay; just notice that bit too.

Hearing the world!

The idea is to become intentional in tuning in to the sounds around you for a period of time: start with the big, obvious sounds, and over time you'll also be able to tune in to the more subtle ones.

Set a timer on your phone for 1 minute, then close your eyes. Tune in to all the sounds you can hear. There might be a bird outside the window, or the sound of the fridge humming in the kitchen; there might be the noise of the bus engine as you read this book on your commute. You'll probably notice that your mind will start to wander to other things, but when this happens, just bring your attention back to the sounds around you. Keep tuning in to more and more sounds until the timer goes off — there will be many more than you think.

Your mind might wander from time to time, and that's okay. Just notice if this happens and bring your attention back to the sounds.

Start perhaps with a minute and work up to about 5 minutes at a time.

The Big 5

This is an extension of listening to sounds as above, except with all your senses. Look around you: what are five things you can see? Four things you can hear? Three things you can smell? Two things you can touch? One thing you can taste? Depending on where you are, some of these might be easier than others. If there isn't anything to taste or smell, just look for more things in the other categories.

Being in your body

Generally, exercises where you notice and connect with your body are called body scans. To do a basic body scan, make sure you're sitting or lying comfortably. Start by focusing your attention on your toes, noticing any sensations in them (wiggle them if you are finding it hard, and just notice that!) — it's important not to judge, just to notice. Then gradually work your way up the body, placing your attention on each part, all the way up to your head. You might find it easier to do this exercise with guided instruction — Google 'body scan' and you'll likely find a whole bunch.

In the earbuds ...

You can make listening to music a very present-focused activity. For instance, when you are listening to a song, tune in on just one instrument (the drums are often a good one to start with). Notice what happens to the beat between the verse and the chorus. Does it form a predictable pattern? Is there a stable beat or does it change constantly?

Doing practical things

Sometimes it can be hard to do the stuff we've chatted about here, but there are other ways that you can practise being present. Try some activities that require you to be completely focused (such as knitting, puzzles, jigsaws, rock climbing). You can also connect with this when you're exercising — you can tune in to the sound of your feet on the path as you walk, for example, or count your steps.

Building a picture in your brain

Sometimes people find it easier to do these exercises if they build up a picture in their brain to imagine. You can either do this yourself (like picturing your favourite place, or replaying a memory, or even a favourite part of a movie) or by getting someone else to help (these are called guided meditations). Again, with this stuff, Google is your friend — look up 'kids meditations' (this is because kids are more visual than young people, but these work just as well for 90 year olds as they do for nine year olds).

Doubling down

You can also put a couple of these together: you could imagine a beautiful place, and then add into it the sensory exercises we chatted about before. Or you could do a breathing exercise before you do any of the others.

This stuff is like finding a comfy pair of shoes: you might need to try out a few before you find the right fit. But this stuff is powerful. Like, magic powerful!

The real stuff

Let me ask you a question and I want you to think about it for a while. Scribble down some thoughts, too — we'll come back to these in a bit!

If I said to you that tomorrow you could do anything you like — but what you did has to feel important to you in some way — what would you come up with?

» Would you use your body in some way? Exercise, swim in the ocean, walk in nature?

» Who would you take with you? Family, friends, other people in your world?

» Would you use your mind? Reading, learning something, challenging yourself with a puzzle or mind bender?

» Would you do something creative? Painting, drawing, writing, building something?

» Would you connect with something in your community? A church, a sporting club, a group of people you could help?

» What would make you feel good about how you spent the day?

» What would you feel a sense of pride over getting done?

How did you go? You might have found it really easy, but most people find they get a bit stuck on some of this, and this might have been one of the harder activities we've done together. Sometimes that's because you haven't thought about it before, or it might be that you don't know exactly what you think feels important. You might have noticed some overwhelm showing up, or even the Anxiety Guy nattering away in your ear. If you skipped over the exercise because it felt too hard, please go back and revisit.

You might also be wondering why I'm asking you to do this (it might seem a bit strange in the midst of all the anxiety stuff). Well, I am so glad you asked!

Imagine that someone said to you, 'I'm going on a cruise ship, and we are going to try to get to Fiji, but there isn't a captain on board.' You probably wouldn't get on that ship, right? You might get to Fiji, sure, or you might end up on Svalbard (a little Arctic island at the top of the world) or you might end up shipwrecked on a reef somewhere.

Sometimes in our lives we find ourselves drifting — like a boat floating around in the middle of the ocean, just going where the tide takes it. Sometimes, that means it might end up where it wants to go, but just as often it will end up somewhere it wasn't intending. But if you get on a boat with a captain steering and navigating, there's a pretty good chance you're going to end up where you set out to go.

And life is the same. But guess what? You are the captain. And it's up to you to work out what's important.

It's often hard for us to identify what the really important stuff is. Life is noisy, and we can end up being pulled by the people around us towards the things *they* think are important. Every person will have different things that feel important, and they will be pulled in different ways towards them.

For most people, the things that are important fall into a few categories:

» *The people around you.* This might be family or friends, or other people you come across in your world. It could be about actual contact and connection, or how you think about connecting with these people — for instance, doing shared activities, looking after someone, sending them things that make them/ you feel nice, or wanting to sit and have a chat with someone.

» *The things you do with your leisure time.* This might include sport, creative activities, or things such as reading or watching TV. It doesn't really matter what these are, it's more about whether you feel they add value to your life.

» *The places you spend your time.* You might really want to engage in the world and be present in the country or near the ocean. You might like to be connected to the world via nature, or you may want to spend time in the built environment, such as walking in the city or visiting art galleries.

» *Things that use your body.* This isn't just about exercise, although that is often important for many people. It might be about things that help you feel you are healthy. Or it could be pushing your physical boundaries to do things that feel hard or learn new ways of using your body.

» *Things that bring you a sense of pleasure.* This is the stuff that feels good — it could be going for a swim, or sewing a quilt. This is as varied as humans are! Everyone has their own preferences.

» *Things that give you some sense of purpose.* This might be learning things, work, chores around the house or even things like making sure the dog is taken for a walk each day.

» *Things that leave your mark.* This might include creative pursuits or using your hands to build something. We like it when we can look at something we have made.

» *Where you live.* This usually involves having connection with the wider community in which you live. You might enjoy being involved in a sporting club or a church, or a service that looks after other people.

Did you notice yourself thinking about some of these? Some of them will be more important for you than others — that's okay, this is your boat that you're steering. It doesn't need to look like anyone else's.

So, you might be still wondering what this has to do with the anxiety stuff.

Well, when anxiety (or other tricky stuff) shows up it can sometimes get in the way of us doing what is important to us. We have had loads of examples through the book about how anxiety might have made you feel that it's too hard for you to go to a party, or to concentrate. So if the thing that's really important to you is human connections and friendships, and anxiety (or other things) gets in the way of that, you are probably not going to feel great.

In the job that I have, I meet lots of people who have really horrible things happen in their lives. And when this stuff happens, they can always tell me what is really important to them (and they often tell me that the things they thought were important aren't so important when something bad happens). You might have had this happen before, where something has happened, and you've realized the true meaning of something.

Knowing what's important won't stop you being anxious. It won't make uncertainty go away. In fact, sometimes making a decision that helps to move you towards your values will bring with it some anxiety and discomfort because you are doing things differently. But what it means is that you are making the decision to do the stuff that is important instead of being pushed around by the anxiety (or other difficult emotions).

Next, we're going to talk about how you can start doing more of the stuff that is important. But before then, I want you to think about where the gaps are for you. What is the stuff that you know is important but which you're just neglecting completely? And what is the stuff that you're nailing?

» What could look different if you were doing more of the stuff that is really important (and not letting Anxiety Guy call the shots)?

» If I was watching a movie of you living that way, what would I see?

» What would change in your mind and body?

» How would you be different in the world around you (people, places or things)?

Doin' what matters

Part of what makes anxiety tricky is that it gets in the way of a bunch of other stuff. So, if Anxiety Guy was just chilling in the back room of the party without anyone else, it would be fine — but that guy is sociable and pulls everyone else in. And sometimes, this also means they pull together stories that make it really hard for us to do the stuff that's important.

We chatted in the last chapter about working out what that stuff is, but it is a totally different thing to actually make steps towards doing stuff. So I'm going to give you an analogy that I sometimes use with young people I see.

Doing stuff when you're anxious is like doing algebra while you're being punched in the face.

There is nothing wrong with your ability to do the algebra, but all your focus and attention goes towards the more pressing thing (which in this absurd example is the being punched in the face bit!).

When anxiety is around, it can make everything else feel really hard and overwhelming, and when you try to focus on something it makes a bit of a swirly mess out of it.

So when we're talking about doing the stuff that is important to you, we have to be a bit smart about it. We know that anxiety is going to show up and start carrying on — Anxiety Guy will be telling you about how everything is going to go wrong, how it's dangerous, etc. We know that story, right? Anxiety Guy is nothing if not predictable (yawn ... come on mate, come up with some new stories already!)

So we know that when you decide to do some stuff that feels important, Anxiety Guy is going to show up. But the stuff you want to do is really important — and there is a cost for not doing it!

Let's do a thought experiment. I want you to scribble down a couple of things:

1. What is something that's important to you that you want to be doing, but aren't doing just yet? (This could be anything: hanging out with friends more, painting/drawing/creative stuff, using your body and getting fit, spending time in nature, etc.)

2. What's getting in the way? What is Anxiety Guy telling you when you think about doing this stuff?

How did you go? How these things were showing up for you might have been really obvious, but remember: sometimes anxiety can be sneaky, so you might have to go digging a little bit if you can't quite see it.

As an example, it might be something like this:

What's important?	Spending time with friends.
What would you like to do?	Go to the parties I get invited to.
What's anxiety telling you?	No one will talk to me.
	I'm going to do/say something stupid.
	Everyone else's outfits will be better than mine.
	There will be loads of people there who I don't know.
	I don't want to drink, and everyone will try to make me (then they'll laugh and call me names).

What's important?	Using my body more.
What would you like to do?	Go to the gym more.
What's anxiety telling you?	I'm not as fit as the other people there and I'll look stupid.
	People will stare at me.
	I don't know how to use the machines properly, and I'll end up hurting myself (which will be painful and embarrassing).

But we now know a bunch of tools to help us manage Anxiety Guy when they show up, right? So let's add another column — this is the one where we think of what the options are to chat about with Anxiety Guy!

What's important?	Spending time with friends.
What would you like to do?	Go to the parties I get invited to.
What's anxiety telling you?	No one will talk to me.
	I'm going to do/say something stupid.
	Everyone else's outfits will be better than mine.
	There will be loads of people there who I don't know.
	I don't want to drink, and everyone will try to make me (then they'll laugh and call me names).
What can you do when this happens?	Thank Anxiety Guy for showing up and trying to keep me safe.
	Notice that Anxiety Guy is trying to pull me into thoughts about all the things that might go wrong. When that happens, remind myself that all those things haven't happened — and come back to the here and now.
	Think about what's important to me: I love hanging out with my friends, and Anxiety Guy has been stopping me going to parties. If I go, I'll probably have a good time, but I know that if I listen to Anxiety Guy I'll be miserable at home.

What's important?	Using my body more.
What would you like to do?	Go to the gym more.
What's anxiety telling you?	I'm not as fit as the other people there and I'll look stupid. People will stare at me. I don't know how to use the machines properly, and I will end up hurting myself (which will be painful and embarrassing).
What can you do when this happens?	Notice that whenever I decide to try something new Anxiety Guy will show up and tell me that something bad will happen. This is really predictable. Notice that I'm getting caught up in the thoughts about the future, but forgetting to think about all the ways it could feel good to go.

How did that feel? What did you notice happening to Anxiety Guy as you thought through this stuff? Did they get louder or quieter? Did they come up with new barriers when you came up with some strategies?

One of the things we know about Anxiety Guy is that they're persistent, right? If you come up with one thing, they will likely show up with something else — this is a good reason to try to not get into an argument with them. Instead, it's much more about noticing that they've shown up, thanking them, and then doing the thing that's important anyway.

It can be important to not jump from 0 to 100 with this stuff. We can go from 'I never go to the gym' to 'I'm a complete failure if I don't go to the gym every single day' in a single thought. So, we want to catch that.

Instead, let's think about baby steps …

In this example, let's be a bit clever about how we think about this. If you go to the gym for the first time thinking that you're going to do a massive session, a few things might happen:

1. You will probably be really sore afterwards (this is actually a good thing, but anxiety will absolutely tell you the opposite!).

2. It might feel too overwhelming to think about going big early, or about doing it again if that's your game plan.

3. Anxiety might talk you out of it before you get there.

This is where the baby steps help. Rather than telling yourself that you're going to go the gym every day for three hours a day from now until eternity (in case you missed it, I'm being dramatic here — this is totally not achievable for most people!), let's instead start with some smaller steps until it feels manageable.

Big Nebulous Goal	Baby Steps Manageable Goal
Going to the gym every day for three hours.	Go to the gym three times this week for 15 minutes at a time (if I want to stay longer when I get there, cool, but start small so it's less overwhelming).
Going to get ripped and buff (or whatever!).	Will do a personal training session that comes with my membership (or watch some videos) to make sure I'm doing things properly.
Running a marathon.	Start by running for 10 minutes on the treadmill and building it up by a small amount each time.

Do you get what I mean?

These things feel way more manageable when we break them down.

I want you to now think about how you can apply this to the stuff you want to do. Think about the important stuff, and then what the goal is. Then break it down, step by step, so that it's something that feels manageable. You might have to do some trial and error — some things will feel easier than others, and sometimes Anxiety Guy will show up more than others. That's okay — they're just doing their job. Remember to thank them, and then go on and do it anyway!

Nighty night

There are two types of people in the world:

1. Those who at some stage in their life have had trouble getting to sleep.

2. Those who at some stage in their life will have trouble getting to sleep.

When we get stressed or anxious, sleep is sometimes the first thing to change (along with appetite) and can be a good indicator that our body is feeling stressed. It's really common that before something big (an exam, a date, a first day at work) we don't sleep so well; the same goes when we're grieving or if something unexpected happens. When this happens, we might have a couple of days of rubbish sleep, but then things will go back to normal.

This will happen to 100 percent of people on Earth at some stage.

But when anxiety is showing up more often, this sleep stuff can get tricky. One of the reasons it shows up at night is that we are trying to keep it at bay during the day (you know, by keeping uber busy so we don't think about it). But it's a bit like holding a ball underwater: at some stage that sucker is going to bounce back up!

These patterns of anxiety/worry showing up in our sleep can get tricky in a few ways:

» We form patterns in behaviour really easily, so if you get into some funny habits of sleeping at strange times (like having a nap when you get home at 5 p.m. because you're tired), you might not be able to get to sleep at 10 p.m. when you usually go to bed. So then you lie awake thinking (probably anxious thoughts!) and not sleeping. So when you're tired the next day, rinse and repeat! Congratulations, you have found yourself in a sleep pattern!

» The stuff your brain tells you as you're trying to go to sleep is likely to be pretty irrational and will seem way worse than it would during the day (thank your 3 a.m. half-awake/half-asleep brain for that!).

» One of the things that is keeping you awake is thinking about not sleeping. You know those thoughts — the conversations that your brain has about how it's only five hours until the alarm goes off, or how you want to be sleeping but can't get to sleep.

The worst thing that happens when you don't sleep is that you don't sleep.

Our brain will tell us a million things that not sleeping will cause — and that in itself can cause us lots of anxiety.

But do you know what happens when you don't sleep?

Nothing.* You might be a bit tired the next day. And maybe because of being tired, you might feel that you're thinking less clearly.

That's it.

So it's interesting, isn't it? We get so caught up in not sleeping that it's often thinking about not sleeping that means we don't sleep!

Yep, I can hear you from here. 'Great. That's really interesting, but what can I do about it?'

I am about to give you some straight-up sleep tips. Some of them you won't like, but sleep is one of the things we can often fix by taking the harder road instead of the easy one ...

1. *Don't be in bed unless you are sleeping!* If you're lying in bed watching Netflix all weekend, your body and brain get confused about when you should be sleeping and when you're lying around being awake time. And yes, before you ask, if you're doing the other thing, you can do that thing in the bed.

2. *Get into a sleep routine.* Our bodies like to have structure, so if you do the same things every night just before bed, your brain

*There is an exception to this rule, which is when you stay awake for more than 72 hours straight. This would usually never happen without input from something external (normally nasty stuff, like being tortured, or artificial things like medications/drugs.). Most people will never bump into this because your body will crash itself out after a long time of being awake.

will clock it and initiate the sleeping sequence. So half an hour or so before you want to go to bed, maybe have a shower or bath, get changed into your jammies, have a cup of tea or whatever works for you. I used to have a patient who would listen to the same album each night before bed. He used to say that he would get about two songs in before he fell asleep. And if he heard those songs at other times, he would get powerfully sleepy!

3. *Put down your devices!* The light and dopamine that we get from our screens is like crack for our brains — and that means they're more stimulated than they need to be (this is also what makes screens so addictive). So, watching TikTok or gaming might mean that you feel sleepy, but it is almost impossible for your brain to relax and switch off. Give yourself at least half an hour before bed when you aren't looking at your phone to let your brain slow down a bit before you ask it to sleep. Also, make sure that you silence your phone when you go to sleep, just to stop the constant pinging which will wake you up a million times a night!

4. *Go analogue.* This is an extension of number 3. The best things we can do to help us sleep are the things we've been doing for ages — things like reading a book (you know, an actual book with pages) or doing a relaxing activity before bed (something with your hands, writing in your journal to reflect on the day, etc.).

5. *When you are thinking about a bunch of things, write them down!* When we're stressed or overwhelmed, most people's brains go into overdrive the second the lights go out. If this happens to you, get a pen and paper (yes, again, an actual pen and paper) and write down your thoughts. Then tell your brain 'Thank you, I'll deal with this is in the morning'. You might need to do this a couple of times, but it helps to put that stuff somewhere else so your brain knows that you won't forget it. My bet is that when you look at

the stuff you've written down the next day, it won't feel nearly as big/overwhelming/scary/hectic as it does at 3 in the morning.

6. *Get your brain to focus on something else.* Our brains are clever, but not clever enough to do two things at once well. So it's hard for our brains to be worrying while thinking about something else at the same time. A couple of ways you can use this to your advantage is to notice that the thoughts, worries or anxiety have shown up and then do some things to get present, like the things we talked about a couple of chapters ago (see pp. 102-106 for a refresher). Or you could do some of the old goodies like counting sheep (this works because your brain has to build a picture of the sheep, and the fence and, you know, all the farmyard vibe). If you don't want to do something like that, it can be really helpful to try to replay the opening scene to your favourite movie. This sounds really simple, but because you've probably seen the movie a few times, your brain will keep jumping ahead. Slow it down and play the scene out frame by frame. The same works with your favourite song.

7. *If you try all of the above, and you still can't sleep — that's okay.* But it probably isn't helpful to be lying in bed and thinking over and over again about unhelpful things. If this is happening, try getting out of bed for a bit, sit somewhere else and read a book (don't look at your screen!!!). You might find that changing the scenery will help to reset things.

Remember, with all of this, your brain is trying to do its job! So, the main thing with the sleep stuff is to not get caught up in the frustration about not sleeping.

It's just that you aren't sleeping.

Thanks, brain!

Sometimes the best thing our brain will hear is something that is a bit unexpected. And it will be really rare that we tell our brains stuff. We listen a whole bunch, but almost never do we return the favour and say something back!

Right about now, you might be wondering exactly what I am on about. Well, there's a really simple thing we can do when our brain is telling us a bunch of stuff (particularly when the message is not to do something). We can just say, 'Thanks, brain'.

Now, this might seem a bit strange after all our talk in the book so far about being present to thoughts, and noticing thoughts as thoughts. Telling your brain 'thank you' is another way of getting distance, because noticing the thoughts is the first step — then it's just a matter of making a choice about what you do. We have already played around with a few of these choices:

1. We have talked about acknowledging thoughts and emotions, and being present to them.

2. We have talked about accepting the emotions and thoughts that show up.

3. We have talked about getting some space and distance from thoughts by noticing them and seeing them as thoughts.

The 'thank you, brain' bit works quite a lot like number 3 in that it is about acknowledging and noticing thoughts. but it's an extension of that. Because saying thank you isn't quite enough.

The next step with the 'thank you, brain' option is the one that's particularly important.

Let's go back a bit and do a thought experiment! How often is your brain saying things like this?

» 'Don't go to school/party/friend's house/work/etc., because the anxiety is too bad.'

» Or: 'I don't feel like exercising/going to school/uni/work etc., so it's better to stay in bed.'

» Or: 'It's too scary out there. Stay here where you're safe.'

» Or: 'Don't raise your hand or ask that question, because you'll look stupid.'

Your brain might have come up with different things, but I think you get what I mean. These are the thoughts where Anxiety Guy (or someone else) tells you to not do things. And they're telling you not to do things out of fear of something bad happening.

This is where the 'thank you, brain' bit comes into play. In thanking your brain, you are recognizing that it has come up with a thought, but you are also recognizing that you don't have to do what that thought is saying. It's the same as when someone tries to hand you something on the street — you might acknowledge them, but you get to decide if you take that thing home (this might look very different if the thing they want you to take home is a bunch of smelly food scraps versus a cute puppy!).

So the next step in this is telling your brain, 'Thank you, brain, but I am going to do it anyway'.

Let's use the example above, about the anxiety being too big to go to your friend's house on a particular day (we know that this is Anxiety Guy's MO, right? They'll often show up to tell you that you aren't able to do a particular thing, or won't cope if you go out — but we know now that this is one of the lies that Anxiety Guy comes up with). When this thought shows up, you have two options:

» You can listen to Anxiety Guy and stay at home. We've talked about this option lots already in the book. When this happens, we know that you're more likely to feel the anxiety get better for a moment, but it will then get bigger the next time that you're faced with the same issue.

» Or the other option is to just do the thing (I know, easy for me to say, harder for you to do!). When we do the thing, it is usually much less bad than Anxiety Guy has told us it would be. And we know now that sometimes hard feelings will show up — but hard feelings show up in scenario one, the first option, as well. But in scenario number two, you get to see your friend.

And in the same way that when you avoid doing something, the anxiety gets bigger, when you don't avoid it, or 'lean into' the hard thing, then the next time you do it the Anxiety Guy won't be so loud, and it will feel easier.

So, I want you to get out your notepad and write down some of the ways your brain is telling you not to do things (or whatever might be showing up for you). And then I want you to write out how the conversation might go, for example:

Anxiety: You shouldn't go to the party, it will make the anxiety worse — and you won't be able to manage it.

You: Thanks, brain. That's a really helpful thought. I see what you're trying to do, and how you're trying to help me. But I am choosing to go to the party.

Anxiety: Really. Well, I'm going to get louder!

You: Thanks for letting me know, brain. But I'm going to make the choice to do the thing that feels harder now, so that it is easier later on.

How did it feel to play that out? I want you to practise that over the next couple of days whenever the Anxiety Guy comes up with reasons to not do something. It might also be that the Anxiety Guy is telling you to do something (but it means missing out on something else — like eating too much because you're uncomfortable, or staying in bed). This works just as well for that.

This will feel a bit weird at first, because my guess is that you've been doing what Anxiety Guy says (and they love it!) and when you start doing things that are different it will feel different (remember the dirt track story on p. 36).

Procrastinating

I'm going to take a stab in the dark and assume that there is someone very familiar to you who's just walked into the party.

Procrastination.

I don't need to introduce you — I suspect you know each other very well indeed. How do I guess this? Well, that's because everyone knows Procrastination. They're like the glitter of the anxiety world (you know how glitter finds its way into everything, even when you haven't used it in months?).

Procrastination is a great trick that anxiety uses to stall us from doing the stuff we need to do, but also the stuff that's important to us. Procrastination is the guy that shows up with a million excuses for why we shouldn't be doing something, and then beats us up when we don't! (Does this sound familiar? This is one of anxiety's lies that we got to know early on, but when it shows up as procrastination sometimes we don't see it so clearly!)

I remember meeting a young woman a few years ago. She was in her final year at school and was struggling with anxiety, but every time she came to see me the same thing was showing up. She had her major artwork due, but she couldn't do it! Every time she started to do some of the work, procrastination and anxiety showed up, and as each week went by the pressure to do something (but also something awesome) got heavier and heavier. Eventually, a couple of weeks before it was due, she threw something together, and she was really unhappy with it. The markers were pretty unhappy as well, and she was devastated when she got her marks back.

But you know what happened then?

Do you think Procrastination Guy was like, 'Awesome job listening to me, mate!'? No, they weren't. They were beating her up, telling her how useless she was and how she should have done the work earlier.

Does this story sound familiar? It might not be something as big as a major work, but procrastination might be showing up in all sorts of things in your life — maybe with work, assignments or homework, but also in putting off doing things that you don't like doing (chores, and things around the house) or life admin stuff. What have you noticed when Procrastination Guy shows up for you?

Most of the time, when Procrastination Guy shows up it doesn't matter too much and the fallout is small. You know, if you put off doing the chores for a couple of hours there probably won't be too much that happens (other than some grumpy parents or housemates). But if you think about it, it's a bit of a false economy (we talked about this back on p. 34 in case you need a refresh). Let's say your chore is to take out the bins. You might spend a lot of time looking at the bins, thinking about how terrible it will be to do the chore, and how much you don't want to do it. But the reality is that taking out the bins will take almost no time to do, and I can guarantee you'll have spent much more time thinking about it. Same with the homework assignments, etc.

> Time spent thinking about a task is way higher than the time it will take to just do it.

Sometimes, though, this procrastination stuff is much nastier and more sinister. It might show up for something really important, where you constantly put off starting a project or an important task despite knowing there will absolutely be consequences for not doing it. Just like the person I used to see with her major work. She was a cracker artist — there was no question that she was going to make something awesome. But because she listened to Procrastination Guy when they showed up, the consequences were big. It was much harder for her to apply to art programs after school, and she then had to do a bunch more work to convince herself (and some other people) that she'd be able to manage when the next big thing came up.

This stuff can also show up with the people we care about. Imagine you tell your friends or your family that you're going to do something that is really important to them. And then Procrastination Guy gets in the way. That's probably going to cause some tension and some fallout.

Remember how earlier in the book we talked about being anxious about being anxious (p. 94). Well, procrastination relies on this. It absolutely assumes

that you're going
to get all caught
up in the thoughts
about the thing, rather
than the thing itself. For
instance, when you look at the
homework question, the thoughts
that show up are more likely to be
about whether you'll be able to do it well,
or whether you know what to do, or whether
other people will do it better, rather than whether
the task itself is easy or hard.

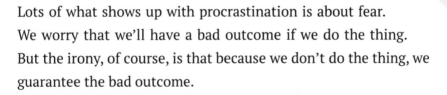

Lots of what shows up with procrastination is about fear. We worry that we'll have a bad outcome if we do the thing. But the irony, of course, is that because we don't do the thing, we guarantee the bad outcome.

So let's think about the major work example. If the person does the major work there are a couple of options:

1. They do something they're really happy with.

2. They create something they would have liked to do differently, but they submit it.

And from there, there are two more options:

1. They get the marks they expected.

2. They get marks that were unexpected (either better or worse).

And so, of course, there is some fear in not getting the marks that they want, or the marks not being as good as they hoped. But it is done, and there are lots of outcomes that may happen as a result.

But if you don't do it, guess what? There is only one outcome.

Sometimes, in order to manage the sense of uncertainty about an outcome, we stop doing anything. This is known as 'uncertainty paralysis'.

Let's do a thought exercise. I want you to think about how procrastination shows up for you:

» How do you know it has arrived?

» What does it stop you doing?

» When it shows up, what are you worried will happen? (Hint: this stuff is often about failure and not being good enough.)

» What tips and tricks have you come up with to help manage it when it shows up?

» Are there particular things that make it worse? (Sometimes this can be about being overwhelmed by a bunch of stuff all at once, and then people get stuck and can't do anything!)

Most of the time procrastination is something that we know we're doing. This arms us with a superpower: we can name it, we can recognize it, and this means we can do something about it!

Throughout the book we've come up with a bunch of tools we can use for anxiety. But it might also be worth experimenting with some of them when Procrastination Guy shows up to see what's a good fit. You might try:

1. Thanking Procrastination Guy for showing up,
   and then deciding to do it anyway.

2. Naming the Procrastination Guy.

3. Thinking about what Procrastination Guy is getting in the way of,
   and what important stuff you're missing out on by listening to them.

4. Coming back to the here and now rather than getting caught up
   in the stories Procrastination Guy is trying to tell you (because we
   know those stories are likely to be pretty rubbish and untrue!).

Which one feels like the best fit for you?

Procrastination might have been showing up for a long time, so you might need to practise a bit on this!

It's got to be perfect ...

So, now we're going to chat about another familiar cat who has shown up to the party.

Perfectionism.

You might know this one as well, but you might not have noticed that it's a separate person. You see, Perfectionism Guy and Procrastination Guy are very good friends indeed.

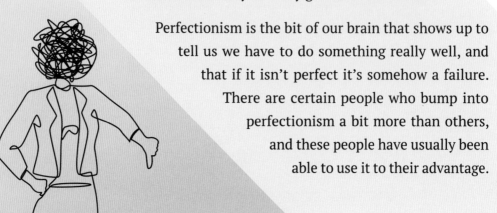

Perfectionism is the bit of our brain that shows up to tell us we have to do something really well, and that if it isn't perfect it's somehow a failure. There are certain people who bump into perfectionism a bit more than others, and these people have usually been able to use it to their advantage.

If perfectionism shows up for you, it might be around the kind of thing that lots of people in your world encourage — getting good marks, putting in loads of effort to be really good at stuff — and you're usually high achieving. You set high targets for yourself, and then you reach them!

So you might be thinking, 'Great! What's the problem with that?' Well, it's kind of a little bit like Spider-Man when he went through that phase of being the bad Spider-Man. (You know the one where he gets the black suit and is all like 'I am Spider-Man, how awesome am I?') The tools that were great for saving the world were really easy to turn against him when used the wrong way.

Think about if someone becomes quite focused on achieving a particular goal in a particular way. It might be that the focus this requires will take up a huge amount of their brain space, meaning they don't have space for other things. All their energy will go into that thing, but then the thoughts about that thing will show up as well (just like when Procrastination Guy shows up).

And perfectionism can be a bit nasty in the things it tells us. It might tell us that if we don't do something to a certain standard we have failed, or even sometimes that the people in our lives will be disappointed in us.

> Perfectionism sets goals that aren't achievable and then beats us up when we don't reach them.

It's a little bit like me beating myself up for not being able to be a professional basketball player. I can show up, and practise and train really hard, but there are some things that will get in the way (like the fact that I'm only 5ft tall and not a natural athlete).

And you know another thing about those lies? Perfectionism is also selling some stuff that isn't true.

So here goes ...

There is no such thing as PERFECT.

It doesn't matter how much you put into something, you will never get to a place where something is perfect. There will always be something you'd want to be different. Sometimes these things are in our control, but most of the time in life you won't have an open-ended amount of time to get something done.

Imagine if your teachers said to you on the first day of school or uni for the year, 'Here's an assignment. You just hand it in when you think it's perfect.' Probably in the moment you'd be thinking, 'Whoot! No due date!' But then, the more you'd think about it, the more overwhelming it would be. How would you know when it was perfect?

My bet is that no one would ever hand that thing in.

That's not how the world works. We have to do things within timeframes and deadlines (both big things and small things!).

Imagine you want your essay to be perfect, so instead of starting the task and getting the words on the page, you either put it off (waiting to make sure you have exactly the right ideas), or you get so lost in the information you need to make sense of that you can't get anything onto the page at all. And in this example, most often people get so caught up in their need for perfection that they don't get it finished at all, and either hand in something that's half-done or don't hand anything in at all. Just like with Procrastination Guy, Perfectionism Guy ends up sabotaging the ways that they could do it well.

Another thought experiment!

> » Do you know when perfectionism is showing up for you?

> » When it shows up, how do you talk to it? Do you go along with it, or do you argue back?

> » Do you get caught in the traps that perfectionism sets? (This might be telling yourself that you need to do more research, or that you need to know all the answers before you start something?)

Perfect doesn't really exist, and if you're putting lots of pressure on yourself to get a 'perfect' outcome, you're likely to fall short, no matter how hard you try.

Just like with Procrastination Guy, we have some choices about how we engage with Perfectionism Guy. We can choose to:

1. do whatever Perfectionism Guy tells us (and deal with the fallout of that when we can't meet the impossible tasks they set us)

2. do what we've done with all the other difficult things anxiety has thrown at us — we can notice the stuff that shows up, and then make decisions about what we do with that!

Just as an example (and some insight into my brain), as I am writing this, those same thoughts have turned up for me. The thoughts that say, 'Your writing is terrible', 'What right do you have to tell people about this? You aren't an expert' and even just 'It's nice outside, why don't you go out into the sunshine? You can write later.' But I know that if I stop writing now, it will be much harder for me to start writing again later. Instead, I have learnt to trick my brain in a bunch of ways:

> » I set myself targets of how many words I will write in a session. Or I commit to working for a set time (I set an alarm on my phone). Today, if you're interested, I'm planning on writing 3000 words — I'm about 2000 in as I write this sentence.

> » I tell myself that the words don't need to be perfect. I just need to get words on the page. I can fix them later.

> » I catch the thoughts that turn up around whether my writing is good or not. I just thank my brain and keep typing.

This has taken practice.

I have loads of bits of writing that I never finished because I didn't think they were good enough. But, by thanking my brain and telling it that I am going to do it anyway, it means that I at least get the words on the page! I write a lot, and the procrastination/perfectionism duo always show up! Talk about predictability.

In the beginning, I would only get a couple of sentences on the blank page before my brain would interrupt me and push me around.

If you get started doing something, your brain will follow. And I am willing to bet that you will feel much better for doing it than not doing it.

Waitin' on a green light

Okay, we're nearly there. We just need to talk about one more lie that anxiety has told us.

Anxiety often tells us to wait for something — it might be telling us to wait for something big to happen, or it might be telling us to wait until the anxiety is better or a certain set of circumstances is reached. It might be telling us we have to wait until something is perfect before we start, or that we can't do one thing until something else (usually something we have no control over) is done! A really simple example of this is when we make resolutions for

New Year. There is absolutely no reason why we can't start doing the thing that's important to us right now, but instead we hold off until the start of the new year.

The Anxiety Guy shows up with a million stories that tell us to do or not do things, and this is an extension of this. When you're thinking of doing something (anything, in some cases) the Anxiety Guy will show up with all the ways that this could go well, or that it could go terribly. We have talked about this loads through the book — but when it comes to decision making it can really get in the way.

I like to think of this a little bit like making the decision not to leave the house until you can guarantee that all the traffic lights to wherever you're going will be green (or if you live somewhere where there aren't traffic lights, it might be something like not seeing another car/animal/tree — very dependent on where you are in the world, but you catch my drift). You can never guarantee this, right? So what we do is that we get up, we get dressed and we leave the house anyway. And sometimes our brain will show up with a bunch of stories about how the traffic is going to be terrible, we're going to be late, etc. But we still leave the house.

So I would like you to apply this to other decisions in your life. It might be that you're holding off studying until a certain set of conditions are reached (the sun's in exactly the right place overhead … you know, that kind of thing!) or that you're going to start doing the stuff that's important tomorrow.

First, notice what is coming up in your mind.

Thank your mind for the suggestion.

Ask yourself, 'Am I waiting for all of the lights to be green?'

If so, think about what you can do differently to move yourself in the direction you want to go.

As we've talked about, things will never be perfect, and while we're waiting for perfection to happen, the time is going to pass anyway!

How you talk to your friends vs yourself!

I want you to think about your best mate (or someone that you're really close to and care about deeply). They come to you and tell you that they're really struggling — perhaps they've been having a hard time, or they tell you the anxiety is making them scared of everything, or even that they're feeling sad all the time.

Now, think about how you would respond. Would you:

a) put your arm around them, listen to them kindly and tell them that they're awesome and that even though it isn't great right now, they're doing the best that they can

or

b) tell them that they're a loser, that they shouldn't be taking up your time, and also probably that they're ugly?

Hopefully, it's obvious what you'd do.

But there's something funny here. When our friends come to us with this kind of thing, we can turn up with kindness and compassion. But we rarely show up for ourselves like this. The whole way through this book we have been thinking about all the ways our brains tell us stories, and how often it is that these stories are untrue, but it's still really hard for us (even when we know about it!) not to hear those messages. And not only do we listen to these messages, we then beat ourselves up for hearing them, or listening and responding to them.

To use our example above, that's like taking option b, and then punching your friend on the face as you walk past. (I don't recommend this BTW.)

So, why do we let ourselves talk to us in a way we would never talk to other people?

The idea of being kind to ourselves (or what we call 'self-compassion' in the psychology business) is something we struggle with. We've already discovered lots of the design flaws our brains have, but one of them is that we are really quick to criticize ourselves (even when we're doing okay!). There aren't many people walking around in the world who have the 'I am the Most Awesome and Perfect Human in the World' Guy showing up, but there are loads of people who have the 'Not Good Enough' Guy, the 'You Could Do Better' Guy and the 'I'm a Loser' Guy (and a million more) showing up.

But just like lots of the other lies, this is also something that our brain tells us that is not even close to being true.

The reality is that we are all showing up the best that we can. That's easier to do when things are going well, but even in the tough times we aren't showing up trying to make things worse.

There is another guy we need to meet, but this guy is one you might feel you haven't met very often. They are quiet and don't often speak, but like lots of people who don't say much, when they do speak it's worth listening to! This guy is the Kind Guy — they are the one who shows up with your friends all the time, but I want you to tune into what they are saying to you.

It's things like:

> » 'Where you are right now is hard.'
>
> » 'You're doing the best you can.'
>
> » 'Anxiety has been pushing you around, but that doesn't mean it's winning. Sometimes it's just bigger than at other times.'
>
> » When life hurts, it's okay to feel things.'

In your notebook, I want you to scribble down any others that come into your mind. What are the things Kind Guy can bring to the party?

I know you're doing whatever you can to try to make your anxiety better (as well as whatever else might be showing up). You aren't waking up in the morning thinking, 'Geez, anxiety, all right I hear you, I'm going to let you blow up my whole life'. No, instead, you are doing the stuff, even when it's hard. You've been doing the exercises in the book, and you're showing up.

So I want you to do an experiment with me. Get out your notepad and find somewhere chill to sit down (ideally without tech or anything that will distract you).

I want you to write a letter to yourself. And in the letter, you are going to reflect on where you are, where you've been, and where you are going! (Don't worry, there are some questions below to help you.) There are a few reasons to do this:

1. Seeing stuff written down has a different weight than when it is in your mind (you are also more likely to believe it!).

2. Focusing on where you are going is helpful in reflecting on where you have been, but also reminds you of all the things you've learnt that have been helpful!

3. It's nice to have something to refer back to if things feel hard sometimes, and you can remind yourself that you're doing the best you can!

So, you can write your own, or you can use the questions below as prompts. This is just for you, so if you would rather draw/paint/make/play something rather than writing, that's fine too!

1. How do you see your anxiety now that is different to how you used to see it?

2. What are some of the things that have changed as you've read through this book?

3. If you were giving advice to your friend about their situation, what would you tell them?

4. What is the stuff you want to spend time on even though anxiety makes it hard sometimes?

5. How do you know that you're doing the stuff that is important?

6. What feels different in your body now? How do you know when anxiety has shown up?

7. How can you include the Kind Guy more? (Remember, they are a bit shyer than the rest of the guys in your brain, so you need to think about how you can make sure they get their two cents in!)

You might write this letter once and keep coming back to it. Or maybe it's something you do over and over again (as your relationship with anxiety changes, the way you think about this stuff might change, too).

Sorry, I thought I heard something just now.

Oh! It's the Kind Guy. They are screaming something! 'Hey you, yes you! You're doing the best you can! I see you. I see how hard it is, but I also see how you are showing up. You got this!'

The quick and dirty: Help in a hurry

These quick and dirty guides are just what they sound like. They're little 'get out of jail free' cards when life has gone from 0 to 100,000 and you aren't sure what to do.

These aren't to fix stuff — they'll just give you some relief from the intensity. Remember, we know that we can't stop tricky things like anxiety showing up, so it's much more about making it manageable.

The idea of these guides is that if something particular comes up (like feeling panicked) you can jump straight into these without having to read a whole chapter.

Sometimes when we feel like the world is unravelling, we just need short snappy info. But I would suggest that if these things are coming up, go back and revisit the relevant chapters once you feel more settled. If stuff comes up once, it might come up again, so revisiting the strategies can be really helpful. And it's always good to practise things when you're feeling okay, rather than waiting until you are feeling out of control. A bit like practising to surf on small waves, rather than paddling out into Pipeline!*

I have tried to think of the most common things that will show up here, but you might have some ideas of your own. If that's the case, think of the things that help and scribble them down in your notebook so you can go back to them when you need them.

*For those who don't know Pipeline, it's a monster wave in Hawaii that's a crazy, crazy hectic surf. Def not for beginners.

When you're panicking (or really anxious)

When we are panicking the best thing we can do is tell our brain that we are okay. We do that by slowing everything down. So:

1. I want you to pay attention to your breathing and really focus on slowing it down.

2. When you breathe in, count to three slowly and then breathe out for three slowly. This is six seconds.

3. Do this ten times.

4. If your brain tries to pull you into thoughts and worries, say, 'Thanks, brain — just going to focus on my breathing now,' and then bring your attention back to your breathing.

5. If after ten times you still feel panicked, keep going until you notice the panic has let up a bit.

6. You might still feel a bit anxious; that's okay. Just notice the feeling of anxiety, and then come back to focusing on your breathing.

Repeat this as many times as you need to.

When you feel overwhelmed

Feeling overwhelmed usually comes from holding too many things in our brains at once, and then starting to spin a bit. Our brain wants us to get caught up in the thoughts, but the best thing we can do is to come back to the present.

1. Bring your focus from your thoughts to the space you are in.

2. Notice five sounds that you can hear — these might be close or far away. They might be human noises or nature noises.

3. Really pay attention to these sounds — try to listen to two at once.

4. If your brain starts to pull you back into the thoughts, notice this is happening and then come back to the space and focus back in on the sounds.

5. Do this for as long as you need for the intensity of the overwhelm to reduce a little.

6. When things feel like they have slowed down in your mind and you're feeling more settled, it can be helpful to write down all the things you're feeling overwhelmed by, then work out which ones you need to do something with and which ones you can put aside for now.

When you feel scared

We all get scared sometimes — and it's okay. Most of the time our brain is telling us a bunch of stuff that makes us scared, but we are actually safe. (However, if you're in physical danger right now, stop reading this and do what you need to do to get out of the situation that you are in.)

1. Notice what you are fearful of. Is it a thought, a worry, or are you thinking about something that hasn't happened?

2. Thank your brain for bringing the thought to your attention, and notice what happens when you do that.

3. Notice what is happening in your body when you're thinking that thought — what's happening to your breathing, where is the fear sitting in your body?

4. Bring attention to that part of your body, and get really curious. What does the fear look like? What colour is it? What happens if you breathe into it, or if you hold your breath? What happens if you imagine it getting bigger or smaller?

5. Now bring your attention back to where you are. Notice all the things around you that tell you you're safe and okay.

When you can't sleep

Everyone has times in their life when they can't sleep. The first thing to realize is that the only thing that happens when you aren't sleeping is that you aren't sleeping. Your brain will tell you a bunch of other stuff, but you are okay.

1. Make sure the room is free of distractions (like phones, laptops, etc.) that will keep you awake.

2. Lie down in bed and notice the feeling of the covers on top of you. (How heavy are they? Are they cool or hot?)

3. Rub your feet together back and forth and notice what this feels like.

4. Close your eyes and imagine a beautiful stream in front of you.* And on that stream there are a bunch of leaves; as each of those leaves float down the stream, I want you to imagine putting a thought onto each of them, and then watching the

leaf and the thought float away. Each time another thought arrives, put that on a leaf and watch it float away too.

5. You might notice that your mind keeps wandering — that's okay, just thank your brain for the wander, and then come back to focusing on the stream. Notice how fewer and fewer thoughts are showing up, but that you might get caught on certain ones — that's okay, just come back to moving them on.

6. If you've done this for a while and you're still not sleeping, get up out of bed and go and get a glass of water.

7. When you come back to bed, try to think of something really boring (like doing your fourteen-times tables, or trying to remember the start of your favourite movie or book).

8. Remember, nothing bad happens if you don't sleep, so just chill. If you spend some time thinking of your favourite movie and not sleeping, that's okay. It's still helpful to be resting in bed.

*This is adapted from an exercise called Leaves on a Stream by Russ Harris (The reference is in the back!)

When you're freaking about social stuff

Sometimes the social stuff catches us unexpectedly. If you're feeling really anxious and panicking when you have to do some social stuff, it can be helpful to feel prepared. So try some of these ideas.

1. Come up with a few topics to have up your sleeve — things like TV shows that you like, or something you've been learning

about. If you get stuck and you feel like you don't know what to say, you can say something like, 'Oh my gosh, I watched the best show the other day — it's called _____ Have you seen it?'

2. Think about some questions to ask the other person — things like, 'What do you like to do on the weekends?' or 'What's the best movie you've ever seen?'

3. If you know that people might ask you a specific question about something (like if you've been unwell or away from school/uni/work) prepare an answer that you can give. This can be as general as you like. Then, go back to asking about them — people love this!

When you're in a social situation and anxiety has shown up:

1. Notice that your brain has pulled you into the stories about anxiety. Thank your brain and then come back to the present. Notice something about the person you're talking to — it might be that they have a nice shirt, or a nice smile. Notice how they're speaking, and really pay attention to their words and how they sound.

2. People love talking about themselves, so ask some of the questions that you prepared. Make sure you pay attention to them and don't get caught up in the stuff your brain might be telling you.

3. Focus on slowing things down — when we get anxious everything tends to speed up. Slow down your breathing, and probably your talking ...

When you're procrastinating

The best thing you can do when you're procrastinating is sometimes really simple (but not easy):

1. Notice that you're procrastinating about something.

2. Notice what your mind is telling you about this thing, and why it is telling you not to do it.

3. Say thank you to your brain.

4. Tell your brain that you're glad it is helping you, but you are going to do it anyway.

5. Think about what you have to do. If the pieces feel too big, break them down until they feel manageable (for instance, if you're doing an assignment, don't think about doing 2000 words right now — just think about doing 50 or 100. And then when you have done those, you can focus on the next 50 or 100).

6. Be kind to yourself if this feels hard. Tell yourself that you're doing the best that you can, but you have to do it even when it's difficult.

7. Celebrate when that thing is done! (You got this! I know that you're going to do it!)

This is not the end ...

Well, it's the end of the book — but it definitely isn't the end of your friendship with anxiety (and all of the other guys that show up).

Now that you're at the end of the book you might feel completely different — or you might feel the same. The anxiety might be showing up less, or you might have noticed that you're noticing it differently. Either way is fine. Like we've talked about, the goal of all of this was never to get rid of anxiety. The goal was always to work out how you can live your life the way you want, even when Anxiety Guy shows up.

Hopefully, through the book you have found some helpful tips — some might be a better fit than others (just like some people love wearing sneakers and some people are all about sandals). The most important thing is to keep going, and to keep working your way along the dirt track to find the beach at the end.

In case it's still hard for you to find the Kind Guy in your brain, I want to mention a couple of things on their behalf.

1. Making it to the end of the book is an achievement. It's hard to think about the way that you think, and to try to change things that feel as natural as how you chew. If you've never thought about anxiety before, then this is massive.

2. Anxiety is hard. Even after reading this book, it might be that it turns up unexpectedly and tries to sucker you into the lies. When that happens, just notice it, and be kind to yourself.

3. You are awesome. (I'm sure that you know this, but it never hurts to hear it from someone else!)

You got this. I can see it from here.

Reference list*

Burckhardt, R., Manicavasagar, V., Batterham, P.J., Hadzi-Pavlovic, D. and Shand, F. 2017, 'Acceptance and commitment therapy universal prevention program for adolescents: A feasibility study', *Child and Adolescent Psychiatry and Mental Health*, 11(1), pp. 1–10.

Dahl, J. and Lundgren, T. 2006, 'Acceptance and commitment therapy (ACT) in the treatment of chronic pain', *Mindfulness-based Treatment Approaches: Clinician's Guide to Evidence Base and Applications*, pp. 285–306.

Dalrymple, K.L. and Herbert, J.D. 2007, 'Acceptance and commitment therapy for generalized social anxiety disorder: A pilot study', *Behavior Modification*, 31(5), pp. 543–68.

Esmaeili, L., Amiri, S., Reza Abedi, M. and Molavi, H. 2018), 'The effect of acceptance and commitment therapy focused on self-compassion on social anxiety of adolescent girls', *Clinical Psychology Studies*, 8(30), pp. 117–37.

Fang, S. and Ding, D. 2020, 'A meta-analysis of the efficacy of acceptance and commitment therapy for children', *Journal of Contextual Behavioral Science*, 15, pp. 225–34.

Halliburton, A.E. and Cooper, L.D. 2015, 'Applications and adaptations of Acceptance and Commitment Therapy (ACT) for adolescents', *Journal of Contextual Behavioral Science*, 4(1), pp. 1–11.

Hancock, K.M., Swain, J., Hainsworth, C.J., Dixon, A.L., Koo, S. and Munro, K. 2018, 'Acceptance and commitment therapy versus cognitive behavior therapy for children with anxiety:

Outcomes of a randomized controlled trial', *Journal of Clinical Child & Adolescent Psychology*, 47(2), pp. 296–311.

Harris, R. 2007, *The Happiness Trap: How to stop struggling and start living*, Exisle Publishing, Dunedin.

Hayes, S.C., Strosahl, K.D. and Wilson, K.G. 1999, *Acceptance and Commitment Therapy*, Guilford Press, New York.

Kohli, M., Gupta, N., Saini, P. and Kohli, G. 2022, 'Comparison of Acceptance and Commitment Therapy (ACT) and Cognitive Behavioural Therapy (CBT) for treatment of academic procrastination', *ECS Transactions*, 107(1), p. 3321.

Neff, K.D. 2011, 'Self-compassion, self-esteem, and well-being', *Social and Personality Psychology Compass*, 5(1), pp. 1–12.

Ong, C.W., Lee, E.B., Krafft, J., Terry, C.L., Barrett, T.S., Levin, M.E. and Twohig, M. P. 2019, 'A randomized controlled trial of acceptance and commitment therapy for clinical perfectionism', *Journal of Obsessive-Compulsive and Related Disorders*, 22, p. 100444.

Salari, N., Khazaie, H., Hosseinian-Far, A., Khaledi-Paveh, B., Ghasemi, H., Mohammadi, M. and Shohaimi, S. 2020, 'The effect of acceptance and commitment therapy on insomnia and sleep quality: A systematic review', *BMC Neurology*, 20, pp. 1–18.

Scarlet, J. 2021, *Super-women: Superhero therapy for women battling anxiety, depression, and trauma*, New Harbinger Publications, Oakland, CA.

Swain, J., Hancock, K., Hainsworth, C. and Bowman, J. 2013, 'Acceptance and commitment therapy in the treatment of anxiety: A systematic review', *Clinical Psychology Review*, 33(8), pp. 965–78.

Twohig, M.P. and Levin, M.E. 2017, 'Acceptance and commitment therapy as a treatment for anxiety and depression: A review', *Psychiatric Clinics*, 40(4), pp. 751–70.

*This is the section where I put all the things that I've read and talked about in the book — you know, just so that you know I'm legit.

Acknowledgements

First up, I just want to say thank you to all the young people I have met over the years who have been willing to share their stories with me! This book has come about because of you.

As always to the Exisle Team — this time around Anouska, Karen, Enni, Beks and Ali — what we have created is better than I could have ever imagined! I look forward to seeing what our next adventure might be!

I have been so lucky to work with an awesome group of clinicians who have not only guided my practice, but who have also provided wise counsel, friendship and have been calm ports in occasionally stormy waters. So, to the Psycho-oncology Team (past and present) and our stellar AYA team — thank you! Catherine Lambert — thank you for allowing me the space and trust to grow in the role, and all of your guidance.

To Iris Bartula, Maree O'Brien and Julie Grove — thanks for your feedback on the early drafts, and your help in crafting the book to where it is now!

We all need some help sometimes — Julie Grove, you always give me the guidance I need at the exact time that I need it, and your skill allows me to hear it.

To the support crew — Gayleen, Ian, Sue, Charlotte, Aaron, Sarah, Iris, Emma, Nicole, Larissa, Cath, Fran, The Surfer Girls, and of course to Renee, you are such an awesome human!

And T. Well, it continues to be one of the most fun journeys one can have!

Index

Index

Index